How to Be a

VALUE
INVESTOR

Other books in the McGraw-Hill Mastering the Market Series

How to Be a Growth Investor
Valerie F. Malter and Stuart P. Kaye

How to Be a Small-Cap Investor
David B. Newton

How to Be a Sector Investor
Larry Hungerford and Steve Hungerford

Essential Guides to Today's Most Popular Investment Strategies

How to Be a VALUE INVESTOR

Lisa Holton

McGraw-Hill

New York   San Francisco   Washington, D.C.   Auckland   Bogotá
Caracas   Lisbon   London   Madrid   Mexico City   Milan
Montreal   New Delhi   San Juan   Singapore
Sydney   Tokyo   Toronto

Library of Congress Cataloging-in-Publication Data

Holton, Lisa.
    How to be a value investor / by Lisa Holton.
      p. cm.
    Includes index.
    ISBN 0-07-079401-4
    1. Investment—Handbooks, manuals, etc. I. Title.
    HG4527.H66   1999
    332.6 — dc21   98-19750
                                         CIP

McGraw-Hill

A Division of The McGraw-Hill Companies

1 2 3 4 5 6 7 8 9 0 DOC/DOC 9 0 9 8 7 6 5 4 3 2 1 0 9

ISBN 0-07-079401-4

The sponsoring editor for this book was Kelli Christiansen, the editing supervisor was Paul R. Sobel, and the production supervisor was Elizabeth J. Strange. It was set in Times Roman per the MMS design by Patricia Caruso of McGraw-Hill's Professional Book Group composition unit.

Printed and bound by R. R. Donnelley & Sons Company.

McGraw-Hill books are available at special quantity discounts to use as premiums and sales promotions, or for use in corporate training programs. For more information, please write to the Director of Special Sales, McGraw-Hill, 11 West 19th Street, New York, NY 10011. Or contact your local bookstore.

This publication is designed to provide accurate and authoritative information in regard to the subject matter covered. It is sold with the understanding that neither the author nor the publisher is engaged in rendering legal, accounting, or other professional service. If legal advice or other expert assistance is required, the services of a competent professional person should be sought.
— From a Declaration of Principles jointly adopted by a Committee of the American Bar Association and a Committee of Publishers.

To Ann Cherepavich Holton

*Mom, thanks for teaching me
that understanding money is
every woman's responsibility.*

CONTENTS

Part Three: Putting It All Together

PREFACE

There's plenty of grumbling among investors about how to find value in a galloping stock market. In fact, that question has been asked incessantly since this unprecedented bull run began more than a decade ago.

But finding undervalued stocks is possible no matter what type of market you're in. In fact, it's best to stop thinking about market swings altogether. It's all a question of gathering the right information, learning some basic rules and calculations, and being coldly objective about where you're placing your hard-earned investment dollars.

That means understanding your tolerance for risk.

If you stopped someone on the street and asked for a basic definition of value investing, they might shrug and give some variation of "buy low, sell high." They're not wrong, in *any* kind of investment strategy, you're looking for bargains that pay off someday.

But value investing, unlike its close partner *growth investing*, is a strategy unto itself and requires its own discipline. A growth investor takes a look at the evidence of product, management, and financial performance and places a bet based on the earnings potential of a particular company, often a very young company. A value investor takes all those things into account, but he or she is looking for something more — a tarnished jewel that others might avoid.

That might mean looking beyond current sales and earnings to peer closely at other financial measuring sticks that tell more about a company's potential than its current prospects.

Sometimes, value investing means looking at companies that are down on their luck or have stock prices that have lagged in the basement for some time. Maybe they've had lousy management, but that might be changing. Maybe their biggest competitor's success is starting to wane. Or perhaps, they are ripe for a buyout which typically raises a stock's price.

At no time in history has the individual investor been in a better position to make competent decisions about his or her money. The explosion of information online (good and reliable sources of information, that is) and in the general media has made it possible for ordinary people to gather the information they need quickly and inexpensively. The whole point is knowing what to look for.

How to Be a Value Investor is a guide to finding information that will help you discover undervalued stocks. But it will also help you understand the same philosophy that professional stock-pickers use when they're running mutual funds. You may never buy individual stocks at any point in your lifetime, but understanding the tools necessary to uncovering valuable investments will serve you well in any investment decision you make.

Information is power. This book is intended to help you find that information and use it wisely.

Lisa Holton

ACKNOWLEDGMENTS

I would like to thank Chuck Jaffe of *The Boston Globe* and Henry Dubroff of *The Denver Business Journal* for recommending me for this project. Colleagues Robin Daughtridge and Kim and Jim DeRogatis were invaluable in reviewing this manuscript and playing the role of beginning investors. Their tough questions have made this book what it is.

Most of all, I thank my sister, Lea Holton, for her encouragement and faith in my work.

How to Be a

VALUE
INVESTOR

Getting Started

The Basics

What Are Value Stocks?

> It doesn't have to be rock bottom to buy it. It has to be selling for less than you think the value of the business is, and it has to be run by honest and able people. But if you can buy into a business for less than it's worth today and you're confident of the management, and you buy into a group of businesses like that, then you're going to make money.[1]
>
> —**WARREN BUFFETT**

How do you define value? Is it a blue light special? Or is it something more a possibility or opportunity that from a distance does not seem so impressive but upon closer observation turns out to be worthy of notice?

Let's go with the latter idea because it fits the purpose of this book. Finding value doesn't just mean buying at cut-rate prices. In rare cases, it might mean spending a little more than you thought you would. Finding value, especially when investing, means making a little discovery that others failed to see, turning it to your advantage, and having your instincts and homework rewarded with a future profit.

A value investor is someone who makes an investment, whether it's a handful of shares or hundreds, using the same thought process it would take to buy the *entire* company. The goal is to buy that company for less than you think it's worth. That means the decision-making process to buy 50 shares in Company A is the same one you would undertake if you were buying Company A lock, stock, and barrel.

This may seem a complicated process. But in truth, it's more time-consuming than complicated and well worth the effort in what you learn. It involves:

- Studying corporate financial reports and using those numbers to give you specific answers.
- Reading everything you can get your hands on about the company you're interested in so you see its bad news as well as its good news.
- Asking the same basic questions you would ask if you were buying an education, a home, or making any major investment: What is this worth now, and will its value increase in the future?

These steps are no different than what the average mogul does when circling a potential takeover target. Moguls always look for a bargain, and the smart ones are willing to spend whatever time it takes to analyze a company before they spend their money.

Why should you be any different? Would you buy a car or a home without inspecting it? Not if you're like most people.

There's another way to describe a value investor; he or she doesn't copy the Joneses. In these turbulent times for the market, that means not worrying about whether the market is up 300 points or down 500 on the day (Figure 1-1).

"It's not always easy to ignore the market, especially when it's jumping all around," admits Barbara Bowles.[2] As founder and chief investment

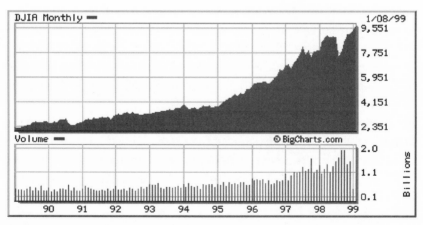

FIGURE 1-1 DJIA Chart 1989–1999. (*Source:* BigCharts.com)

manager for the Chicago-based Kenwood Group, which operates the Kenwood Growth and Income Fund, a mid-cap value fund, she decides where to invest more than $2.5 million each day. Bowles continues, "But looking for value means looking closely at a company, not the market or the herd mentality you see around it."

Peter Lynch, the Fidelity Investments guru who has made a career out of preaching the benefits of assessing investments on a close, individual basis puts it this way: "What you're asking here is what makes a company valuable, and why it will be more valuable tomorrow than it is today. There are many theories, but to me, it always comes down to earnings and assets. Especially earnings."[3]

Simply put, value investing is a well-researched bet that pays off nicely in the long run, and it doesn't matter if you are a large or small investor when you begin.

What's the Difference Between Value Investing and Growth Investing?

It's semantics, mostly, but value investors are different from growth investors in that they demand more of a track record from their companies. Here's an example. By year's end 1998, Amazon.com, the online book and music store, was trading at a 52-week high of around $160 a share (after a 3-for-1 stock split) and 52-week low of $18.25. That's quite a spread. Most people who watch Amazon.com say it's a heck of a growth stock.

However, the value investor needs to know a lot more, particularly about the assets and the earnings stream of the company.

Amazon.com has been public since 1997 and had a whopping 840 percent increase in annual revenues that first year, but it has yet to turn a year-end profit. Growth investors would note how sales are continuing to grow and business is expanding, but with a "nonmaterial or meaningless" P/E ratio, since the company isn't posting earnings, many conservative investors might wonder what the value of the company really is (Figure 1-2).

As 1998 wound to a close, the debate about Amazon.com's value only got hotter. With Amazon trading at a lofty 97.4 times sales, a figure many like to compare to top U.S. retailer Wal-Mart's trading price of 1.6 times sales, Henry Blodgett, a stock analyst at CIBC Oppenheimer in New York, declared that Amazon stock would reach $400 a share during 1999

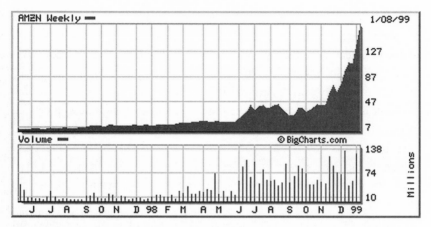

FIGURE 1-2 Amazon.com Chart 1997–1999. (*Source:* BigCharts.com)

(see Figure 1-3). Essentially, that $400-a-share target was met when the company split its stock in January 1999. But other analysts have decried Blodgett's opinion, asserting that the stock would eventually fall below $100 a share once investors started to properly examine Amazon's fundamentals.

There's an old investing legend that several experts have brought up in reference to the Amazon.com saga. It is the story of the tulip bulb frenzy of 1634, when Dutch speculators bid the price of tulip bulbs sky-high only to see them come crashing down again. Many people suggest that's what the stampede toward still-unproven Internet stocks has been during the past year—a form of "tulipmania" bound to fail because the underlying fundamentals of these stocks don't justify their high prices.

And determining fundamentals is what the value investor's decision-making process is all about.

So Who Came Up with This Value Idea Anyway?

If you're a beginning investor or if you've remained awake through a few college courses on finance and market theory, you might have heard the name Benjamin Graham (1894–1976). Every philosophy has to have a granddaddy, and for value investors, Graham's the guy.

Two of his books, *Security Analysis*[4] and *The Intelligent Investor*,[5] have been bibles for thousands of beginning investors. Neither is particularly easy

Company	Market Value (in billions)	Revenue Estimates (in billions)
AMAZON.COM	$11.1	$0.542
MATTEL	10.1	5.2
FEDERATED DEPT. STORES	8.5	15.8
DELTA AIR LINES	7.9	14.6
HERSHEY FOODS	7.6	4.5
KMART	7.5	33.7
HILTON HOTELS	5.6	5.5
TOYS 'Я' US	5.2	11.4
MAYTAG	4.9	4.2
APPLE COMPUTER	4.6	6.9
CIRCUIT CITY	3.7	9.3
BARNES & NOBLE	2.2	3.1

Market valuations as of Dec. 1, 1998.

Source: Business Week, Dec. 14, 1998, using Bloomberg analysts' estimates.

FIGURE 1-3 Market value vs. performance estimates: Where the market goes, will reality follow?

reading, but Graham asks the central question that all investors should ask: Before you invest your money, do you know what your investment is worth?

Graham was a stickler for valuing the assets of a company, which in his day were certainly more tangible things like equipment, real estate, buildings, and cash. Yet he wasn't an absolutist about bricks and mortar:

> A stock does not become a sound investment merely because it can be bought at close to its asset value. The investor should demand, in addition, a satisfactory ratio of earnings to price, a sufficiently strong financial position, and the prospect that its earnings will at least be maintained over the years. This may appear like demanding a lot from a modestly priced stock, but the prescription is not hard to fill under all but dangerously high market conditions.[6]

Much of this seems like common sense. So how did this guy get so famous for coming up with something most people could figure out on their own?

It's because Graham—and his most famous disciple, Warren Buffett of Berkshire Hathaway Corp.[7]—have promoted a specific method for making numbers tell a story. It involves looking behind the price of a stock, which might be skyrocketing or taking a dive, and finding out what the actual investment is worth and what its potential is for future gains. Since this book will deal primarily with equities (stocks), let's start by asking some of the questions that Graham and his followers would ask about a particular company's stock.

- Forgetting where the stock is trading for a moment, what does this company make, and what does it own that could be sold off right now, for cash? In other words, what are its assets?

- What does this company owe? Is it in hock to an army of creditors, or does it have low debt and a fair amount of cash in reserve?

- Is the company any good at what it does? Who says so? What does its competition look like?

- Is this company earning money? If its profits have fallen lately, is it because they had a little bit of bad news or horrible problems that will take time to fix—and may not be fixed at all?

These are questions that anyone might ask. But there are specific tools to find those answers.

Some of these tools are mathematical. If you thought you left formulas behind in high school algebra, get ready to deal with them again. You'll be learning the definition and use of price/earnings ratios, price-to-book value, corporate tax rates, and other financial guideposts that all public companies share. You will also learn how investment experts follow some of these guideposts devotedly and discard or refine others, depending on their approach to investing.

Examining numbers and doing computations outside of the simple addition and subtraction involved with gains and losses scares a lot of people. Don't let these formulas and ratios scare you. They have a very clear purpose, they're not hard to understand, and once you see their relevance, you'll use them often.

The best part: you do get to cheat a little. You'll find some of these computations already done for you in your morning newspaper. And there are leading-edge investment services, such as Value Line and Zack's Investors Service, that offer you these computations ready-made over many years so you can get a long-term view of a company's performance. All of this information is as close as a click on the computer or a quick trip to your public library. In Chapter 3, you'll find a quick listing of definitions, the formulas, and how to compute them. And in Chapters 9 and 10, you'll get a wealth of resources to find at the library, your local bookstore, and online.

Will this book encourage you to follow Graham's philosophy to the letter?

No.

As mentioned above, many investment professionals who call themselves value stock-pickers don't follow Graham to the letter either, mostly because times change. Plenty of them would say Graham's toolbox is pretty obsolete in some areas, pointing to his reliance on book value, a historical measurement of assets that some would argue doesn't indicate what a company is worth *today.*

Just remember, such debate shouldn't unnerve you as an investor. It should strengthen your resolve to learn more. Seeing what these competing approaches are and how well they work will help you develop your own instincts and attitudes about finding value in the marketplace.

Start Filling Your Toolbox

An investor needs resources to think with. The book in your hands right now is only a small fraction of what you'll need to start your search for value stocks. In succeeding chapters, we'll talk about how to use your daily newspaper, your local library, and your computer to help you find value in your investments.

The computer, through the growth of resources on the Internet and software that can help you analyze investment data quickly, is perhaps the most fertile area for investors to do research. Lots of new and interesting tools are being added every day. But it's important to realize that not everyone has a computer or feels comfortable working on one, so this book seeks to tell you how you can work without a computer to find the information you'll need.

The Current Market Environment

You'll hear a lot in this book about how value stock-picking should have nothing to do with whatever craziness is going on with the market as a whole. In fact, as the first words of this book were being written, the Dow Jones industrial average was approaching an all-time high of 9383. By the time the first draft was completed, the DJIA had slid more than 1000 points and given up all of its gains for the year so far. Even value mutual funds took a hit during the July–October slump. According to Chicago-based Morningstar Inc., the mutual fund research and rating house, the average value fund lost 23 percent from July 17 through October 8, more than the decline of the S&P 500 during that volatile period.

But by the second draft, the Dow had not only regained its autumn losses, it had surpassed the 9600 mark. Yet value stocks didn't mimic the Dow's heady recovery. By the end of the year, large-cap value funds finished with a 12-percent gain for the year, mid-cap value funds showed a gain of only 1.4 percent and small-cap value funds, an actual loss of 6.65 percent.

So it might be best not to assume the market will raise all boats equally.

Yet the overall market *does* have an impact on value stocks in one significant way: When the overall market is rocketing, it's tough to find a *lot* of stocks with the fundamentals and earnings news that might trigger your bargain search. When the market goes down, there are more stocks approaching value levels. It's as simple as that.

The most important point: The overall market shouldn't change your approach to finding good stocks. It just makes the search a little tougher—or a little easier.

Patience Is a Virtue

Before moving on, it makes sense to discuss what probably brought you to this book in the first place: a desire to see a profit as soon as possible after an unprecedented 10-year bull run in the stock market.

Not so fast.

A word of caution: value investors don't often see quick profits. Many of the companies value investors buy are older firms having short-term earnings trouble that takes time to work out. Maybe other investors haven't caught on to the potential *you* know is there. Investment professionals who buy stocks from a value strategy will tell you they often hold a stock anywhere from two to five years before they take a well-deserved profit—or bail out with greater wisdom and a loss.

Laura Sloate of the Milwaukee-based Strong Value Fund points out one of her key requirements in buying value stocks: "Value will emerge only in a sea of bad news," she says. "If you see bad news or trouble signs on the way, that's the time to spot value—you do your homework, you trust your numbers, and then you watch."

So the concept of "buy and hold" really does fit the value investor. However, buy and hold doesn't mean "sit and ignore." Using the processes and tools detailed in later chapters, you will be able to confirm your selections at regular intervals and wait for a profit with confidence.

CHAPTER 2

What's on Special?

How the Experts Search for Bargains

Don't gamble; take all your savings and buy some good
stock and hold it till it goes up, then sell it. If it don't go
up, don't buy it.

—WILL ROGERS

I f only life were that simple. Short of finding a crystal ball, stock-picking is an inexact science for even the most experienced people with the best data and training in the world. No investment professional will tell you she or he is right 100 percent of the time, and those who specialize in value haven't had much good news in the last two to three years, since the DJIA and other indexes of stock performance have climbed to all-time highs (Figures 2-1 and 2-2).

The adage of a high tide lifting all boats has great resonance in the stock market. It makes finding a bargain tough. After all, when the market goes up—and keeps going up—the way it has for the past ten years, what's the point of you, the investor, doing homework? You can just go along for the ride, right? That sentiment has created unprecedented interest among individual investors in the stock market. Benefits consulting firm Hewitt Associates estimates that 401(k) retirement plan assets of over a trillion dollars represents the largest pool of money invested in capital markets today.[1]

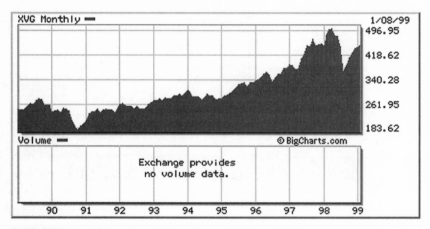

FIGURE 2-1 Value Line Index Chart 1989–1999. (*Source:* BigCharts.com)

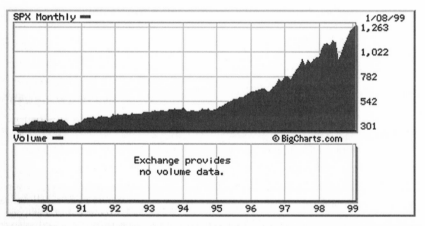

FIGURE 2-2 S&P 500 Chart 1989–1999. (*Source:* BigCharts.com)

However, the market runup has made die-hard value investors the "May-tag repairmen" of the nineties market world. No one really takes a bargain-hunter seriously when the market continues to take portfolios skyward. Besides, these professionals tend to focus on wounded companies, and in a market upturn, most eyes are on sexy growth companies with plenty of potential but without earnings and performance record value investors demand in order to make their decisions.

Therefore, Warren Buffett has counted himself in the minority. "I have seen no trend toward value investing in the 35 years I've practiced it.

More Than One-Third of Your Investment Dollars Are Going Toward Retirement

The Investment Company Institute (ICI), the mutual fund industry's largest trade group, estimated that as of 1997:

- The retirement share of mutual fund assets in 1997 remained near 35 percent for the fourth consecutive year.

- While the retirement portion of mutual fund assets remained stable, mutual funds' share of total U.S. retirement assets grew modestly. Mutual fund assets in retirement plans rose 28 percent in 1997 to $1.6 trillion, giving the industry a 17-percent share of the $9.4 trillion U.S. retirement market, up from 16 percent the year before.

Source: ICI, July 13, 1998.

There seems to be some perverse human characteristic that likes to make easy things difficult."[2]

Value investors tend to be killjoys in a major market upturn—most wonder aloud why people are buying certain stocks at 20, 30, 40 times earnings when with a little work they can find promising companies that are much cheaper overall.

What the Pros Do

FUND MANAGER SNAPSHOT

David A. Katz, **portfolio manager for the Matrix/LMX Value Fund** Ticker Symbol: **LMHFX** Fund Family: **Matrix/LMH Value Fund** Address: **444 Madison Ave., Ste. 302, New York, NY 10022. 800-366-6223**

Katz's Strategy: **Buy good businesses with strong balance sheets that are inexpensive based on their peer group of companies. The company must have a dividend and earnings stream of several years, and book value, price to equity, and return on equity are also analyzed.**

Tools Used: **Katz uses various custom computer models to sift through companies, but like many of his peers, he uses various**

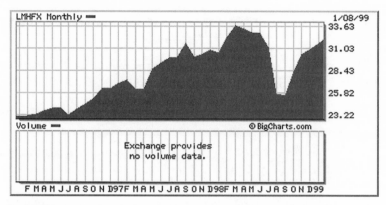

FIGURE 2-3 Matrix/LMX Performance Chart. (*Source:* BigCharts.com)

online search engines and newswires to ferret out news of change—preferably negative—in a company's operations. He also has access to Value Line reports, commonly found in public libraries everywhere.

David Katz, chief investment officer for the Matrix/LMH Value Fund (Figure 2-3) was rubbing his hands together recently when nervousness about the world economy and possible impeachment proceedings against President Clinton loomed in the air. It's not that Katz and his brethren live for bad news, but they do live for reality checks:

> We've just gotten through the most difficult period for value invest-ments in the last 20 years. Pure low price/earnings ratios have been the worst in three decades, meaning they've been abnormally high. We've seen a blind focus on current quarterly earnings, and trouble signs get ignored. But that can't last forever, Katz said.[3]

Katz sees the best opportunities in what he calls "the broader market," companies ranging in size from $200 million to $10 billion with annual revenues. "What it excludes are the Lucents [Lucent Technologies] of the world, which are good companies but entirely too richly priced." He's referring to Lucent's nonmaterial (too high to be relevant) P/E ratio at the end of 1998 (Figure 2-4).

Katz looks for stocks with great brand names and solid market leader-ship that have been battered.

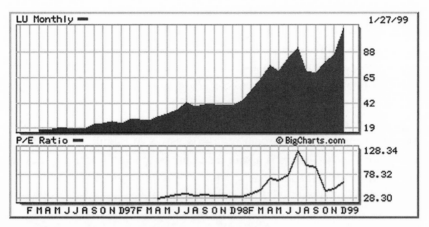

FIGURE 2-4 **Lucent Technologies Chart.** (*Source:* BigCharts.com)

One is Eastman Kodak: "This is a company that is halfway through working out. In 1997 they had competitive problems with Fuji Film, and the company has been written off as a dying business. They were selling at 14 times earnings when the rest of the peer group was selling at 28. But we realized they had 68-percent market share and a world-recognized brand. I figure they're halfway through their workout, but we're sticking with them."

By year's end 1998, Kodak was selling at nearly 62 times earnings (Figure 2-5).

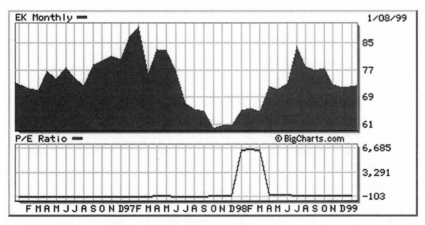

FIGURE 2-5 **Eastman Kodak Chart.** (*Source:* BigCharts.com)

Katz's fund, like the rest of the fund industry, depends on computers to help discover stocks that might be candidates for purchase. "We have six business models, and we require they score on two of all six," he says. Those measurements include earnings growth, dividend stream, price-to-book value and price to cash flow (more on these definitions in Chapter 3).

"We use a price-to-book value measurement based on return on assets. If a company has a 20-percent return on assets, we think it is worth 2.5 times book value, which is a safe place for us to start examining a company more closely," Katz adds.

On the qualitative side, Katz says he looks for a number of good signs: "You want to make sure they're a strong player in their industry and that management tends to be a strong shareholder. It's a nice thing to see inside buying."

RESEARCH TIP:

Where can you find some of the information that Katz uses? For key ratios here, go online to www.valueline.com or to your local public library for the printed Value Line investment reports on the company you're researching.

When does he sell? Katz says the normal holding period for a stock in his fund is between 18 and 36 months, and the sale target range comes into focus when the price of the stock meets Katz's initial price estimate for value.

What are the best value sectors in 1999? "Watch companies that have really been knocked down for their Asia exposure ... there is growing value in the semiconductor area, automotive-related industries, oil drilling, and electronics wholesalers."

FUND MANAGER SNAPSHOT

Barbara L. Bowles, portfolio manager for the Kenwood Growth and Income Fund Ticker Symbol: **KNWDX** Fund Family: **Kenwood Funds** Address: **10 S. LaSalle Street, Suite 3610, Chicago, IL 60603. 312-368-1666**

Bowles's Strategy: Bowles sees herself as a bottom-up investor, which means taking a hard look at the company's financial history and placement in its industry before any projections begin.

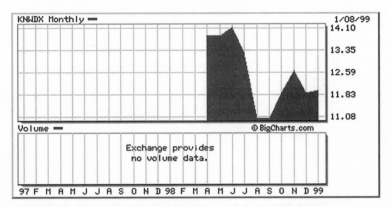

FIGURE 2-6 Kenwood Fund Chart. (*Source:* BigCharts.com)

Tools Used: **Bowles looks for a low price-to-book ratio against the rest of the company's industry peers; a low price-to-earnings ratio against its industry peers; and a strong cash flow, as opposed to low debt.**

Barbara Bowles already had a long career in investor relations and investment policy at Kraft Inc. and Beatrice Companies before starting her own Chicago investment firm in 1989.[4] Today, her Kenwood Group manages pension funds for such corporate customers as Quaker Oats, Abbott Laboratories, and the City of Atlanta, and her fund for average investors, the new Kenwood Growth and Income fund, was bouncing back late last year after the overall market tumble in August and September (Figure 2-6).

"We find value when people give up," says Bowles. Misfortunes that draw Bowles's interest might range from a short-term hit to earnings or a mistake like a product disappointment. The key is to find out how big the problem is, when it can be solved and if management is up to solving it.

"We always look at the balance sheet to see how much cash this business is throwing off and then we look at the business plan. Does this company have a leading edge in one of its products or a niche that no one else is filling?" asks Bowles. "We're always happy with a No. 1 company in a less-known industry."

An example is DSC Communications, a telecommunications company purchased by Bowles's fund roughly three years ago. The maker of telecommunications equipment was purchased in June by a French company, Alcatel, which is a nice way for a value story to end—in a takeover (see Figure 2-7).

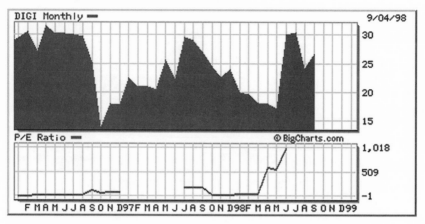

FIGURE 2-7 DSC Communications Chart 1996–1998. (*Source:* BigCharts.com)

"If you're a value company, you need to be patient with your investment, or you need a catalyst to realize it. With DSC, we didn't count on a takeover, but it was a nice catalyst toward realizing our value," said Bowles.

Another proud value acquisition that Bowles made in 1990 for her institutional clients was Citicorp, then struggling at $10 a share as financial problems in Hong Kong damaged its results (she has long since eliminated the stock from her picks). "Results [at that time] were horrible, but we decided that Citicorp was a global brand with a poor industry P/E value. While most of the signals were quite negative, we felt the Hong Kong government was going to be fine and Citicorp would gain more ground globally. Sometimes you have to shut your eyes and go with your gut, but it was based on signals we believed would turn around. And they did."

Not only did Citicorp turn around during the 1990s, it signed one of the major financial merger agreements in history during 1998, agreeing to merge with Travelers' Group for over $70 billion (Figure 2-8).

For an example of a value play in a cyclical industry (one that depends on cycles of demand among its key consumers), Bowles points to Cummins Engine, a Chicago-based maker of diesel engines: "Right now, they're coming down from highs because their earnings have peaked in a cycle."

Cyclical industries—automobiles and automobile equipment, farm equipment, steel—are worth getting to know not for their peaks, but for

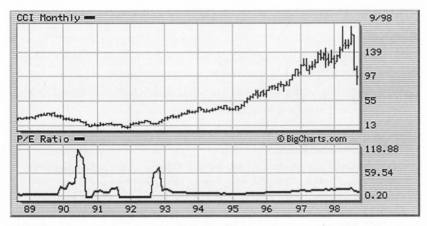

FIGURE 2-8 Citicorp One-Decade Chart. (*Source:* BigCharts.com)

their valleys, Bowles points out. It also makes sense to look at how other companies in their peer group are doing (another piece of data that can be found on Value Line or the personal finance pages of America Online or CompuServe).

That's also why Cummins looked good at mid-year 1998, she said: "We like to buy when the stock price is roughly 30 percent under the fair valuation we judge for the stock. … At this point in time, we see Cummins as a value and a bargain." (See Figure 2-9.)

Does the economy matter? In the case of naturally cyclical stocks, yes, Bowles says. But only to the extent "it throws the cycle out of whack, and

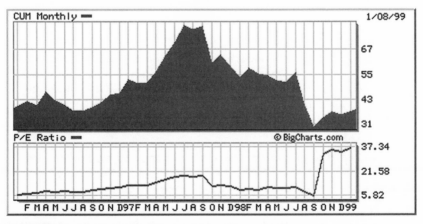

FIGURE 2-9 Cummins Engine One-Decade Chart.
(*Source:* BigCharts.com)

then, it's really an issue for the entire peer group, so the playing field adjusts."

When does she sell? Typically within a 24- to 30-month time range, Bowles says. "The last 12 months haven't been great for value, but for the last six months, it's outperformed growth. Historically, value slightly outperforms growth over the long term."[5]

FUND MANAGER SNAPSHOT

Jim Oberweis, **portfolio manager for the Oberweis Emerging Growth Fund** Ticker Symbol: **OBEGX** Fund Family: **Oberweis Funds** Address: **951 Ice Cream Drive, Suite 200, North Aurora, IL 60542.** Tenure: **11 years. 800-323-6166**

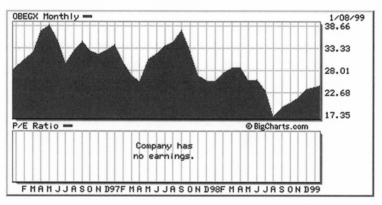

FIGURE 2-10 Oberweis Growth One-Decade Chart. (*Source:* BigCharts.com)

Oberweis's Strategy: **His fund is officially considered a growth fund, not a value fund, but Oberweis says, "We consider ourselves value investors of growth stocks." The fund normally invests at least 80 percent of assets in companies that are among the smallest 30 percent by capitalization of major stock exchanges.**

Tools Used: **Heavy research in companies having a strong product and good revenue and earnings potential with good price/earnings and price/sales ratios. "Unflawed" balance sheets a must.**

Jim Oberweis, head of a family that made its name in ice cream (the famous Oberweis dairy of Aurora, Il.), is also a long-time name in investment.[6] Yet last year, he was not in the best of moods. At mid-year 1998, Oberweis was attempting to steer through a two-year downturn in small-company growth stocks and was not sounding particularly bullish (Figure 2-10).

Oberweis has taken to waving around a 1974 *Wall Street Journal* "Heard on the Street" column declaring the over-the-counter (small-company, small-cap) stock market "a disaster." "It's a lot like what we're seeing today. Since the start of the year, the Russell 2000 [a leading index for small-capitalization stocks] has been off 18 percent, though it was down more earlier in the year."

But how is Oberweis feeling? Like a buyer. "The value investor looks primarily at assets, and the growth investor looks at potential. I think we've got a little more value than we had, and I think the overall economic picture is good enough to provide the potential," he notes.

Now may be a good opportunity for patient investors to pick up some values in the marketplace among small-company stocks that—at least in recent history—have outpaced large-company stocks.

Large Company vs. Small Company Performance (1975–1983)		
Year	**Large Company Returns**	**Small Company Returns**
1975	37%	53%
1976	24%	57%
1977	−7%	25%
1978	7%	23%
1979	18%	44%
1980	32%	40%
1981	−5%	14%
1982	21%	28%
1983	23%	40%

Source: Ibbotsen Associates/Bloomberg News.

The P/E ratio for the S&P 500 between 1928 (the year before the crash that heralded the Great Depression) and today has averaged 14.6. By

Year	P/E
1935	17.22
1940	10.21
1945	18.08
1950	7.19
1955	12.56
1960	17.76
1965	17.58
1970	17.27
1975	11.87
1980	9.19
1985	13.78
1990	15.21
1995	17.47
1997	23.99
1998*	27.55

*As of September 15, 1998

FIGURE 2-11 S&P 500 P/E Chart. (*Source:* Global Financial Data, Alhambra, CA.)

year's end 1998, the S&P 500's P/E stood at roughly 27.55. A recent article in *Esquire* magazine points out that in 1985, a dollar of earnings from a NASDAQ stock would have cost an investor $19.23. As of September 1998, a dollar of earnings from a company in that technology-heavy index cost roughly $86.62.[7] Figure 2-11 tells the story.

"The P/E for the S&P 500 is at historically high levels, and to me, it's reminiscent of 1973, when you had stocks like Polaroid and Xerox selling at huge multiples. Meantime, small stocks have been in a one-to-two-year bear market. I think there's some opportunity here," says Oberweis.

INVESTMENT MANAGER SNAPSHOT

William B. Hummer, **principal and market economist, Wayne Hummer Investments LLC, Chicago. 800-621-4477**

Hummer's Strategy: **Looking for out-of-fashion investments.**

Tools Used: **P/Es, dividend yields at a discount to industry peers.**

Bill Hummer, a former U.S. Army counterintelligence officer, brings a certain amount of that skill to his job managing the family investment firm.[8]

Although not a fund manager, Hummer's abilities as a Chicago-area stock-picker are well known. He participates in *The Wall Street Journal's* semiannual economic forecasting survey, is a former member of *The Chicago Sun-Times* "Picks of the Pros" panel and is one of the economists surveyed quarterly by the Federal Reserve Bank of Philadelphia.

The Princeton-educated economist stays away from computer models and sticks to guideposts most individual investors have easy access to. He studies the Value Line numbers carefully and watches the health of cyclical and noncyclical industries very closely. He reads local and national newspapers and business magazines to make sure he knows the latest news on companies he's curious about.

He also keeps abreast of brokerage analysts who seem to have the inside track on various companies and are most reliable with their projections.

"There are many specialists throughout the investment community, and you have to search for the best brains to get your information," explains Hummer. "It's actually a wonderful time because with the Internet, you can find out what just about everyone is saying without having to read about it secondhand."

RESEARCH TIP: WHERE TO FIND THIS RESEARCH

Analysts' reports are put out by investment firms for their clients. However, there are many free sources of this research, primarily through the Internet. America Online's financial page allows users to access research reports on thousands of stocks. Zacks' Investment Service also allows free access to so-called analysts' estimates, which are Zacks' own averages of earnings projections for companies.

Hummer also looks at the banking industry very closely and is therefore plugged in to the Asian, Russian, and Latin American financial crises that jumbled the markets in the summer of 1998. Even Hummer wasn't sure exactly how the "Asian contagion" would affect markets going into 1999, so he started advising his firm's investors to take a closer look at stocks that represented consumers' needs instead of wants—utilities, energy, and telecommunications, to name a few.

And in times of uncertainty, he also notes that investors should get back to the practice of measuring assets, not growth potential, as a starting point for investment. "I think book value has been denigrated too long as a measurement of what a business is worth," he explains. "I know in some industries it is a tremendous measurement—banking for one—and less so in others, the Internet being the best example. But the bottom line is that investors need to do more homework to figure out where they're putting their money."

The search for value at Wayne Hummer has led to a range of stock picks that Bill Hummer is willing to share, and it may be a shock to some investors that they're not all that cheap. Hummer stresses that value doesn't always mean uncovering a stock at under $20 a share. Sometimes it means finding a jewel whose value has yet to be fully realized, even if the market is already behind it.

Such a pick would be Cisco Systems, a company that creates systems to link computer equipment for the Internet (Figure 2-12). Hummer stresses that while he fails to understand the value behind many Internet "content" companies (search engine and portal companies like Yahoo! and America Online), he knows the Internet is here to stay, "and somebody has to make sure it works."

SBC Communications is another Hummer pick because its acquisition trail will allow it to pick up Ameritech, the Midwestern Bell operat-

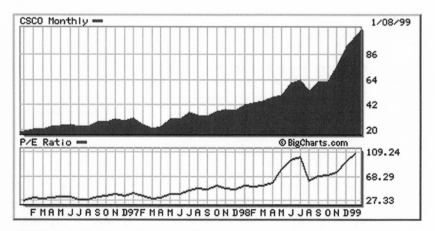

FIGURE 2-12 Cisco Systems Chart. (*Source:* BigCharts.com)

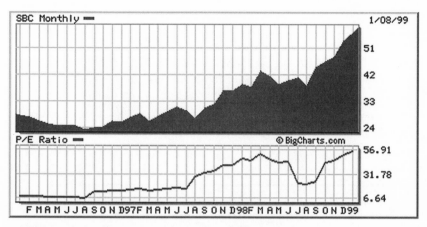

FIGURE 2-13 SBC Communications Chart. (*Source:* BigCharts.com)

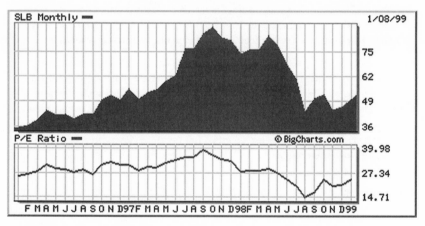

FIGURE 2-14 Schlumberger Chart. (*Source:* BigCharts.com)

ing company (Figure 2-13). The $61-billion deal is expected to depress earnings. Depressed earnings typically depress stock prices.

Hummer also feels the uncertainty of world markets will put a floor on falling oil prices and that will help oil-field service companies like Schlumberger Ltd. (Figure 2-14). Higher oil prices increase oil company revenue and strengthen demand for exploration and production products and services.

INVESTMENT MANAGER SNAPSHOT

John Rogers, **President, Ariel Funds, Chicago. 312-726-0140**

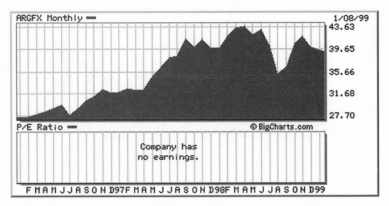

FIGURE 2-15 **Ariel Growth Fund Performance.** (*Source:* BigCharts.com)

Rogers's Strategy: **Typically looks for small-cap companies of $1.5 billion (in market capitalization) or less with P/E ratios of less than 15. Stays away from heavy-duty cyclical industries in his search for companies.**

Tools Used: **Professional databases to keep abreast of news on the companies he and his managers are watching. He also uses the Internet search engines to find any other information the databases might have missed. He and his managers spend a lot of time on the phone with other investment managers to get a full array of viewpoints on a company before investing.**

John Rogers has taken a lot of heat in recent years for his conservative stance on the market. He has believed the market has been overvalued for at least the last three years.[9] (See Figure 2-15.)

But after a summer of downturns in the overall market, Rogers modestly stated, "I feel a little vindication right now. I think I'm going to feel more later. My hope is for a real flight to quality, not just quick profits."

For an investment manager who advertises his main fund as a "growth" investment, Rogers is really a value player all the way. He avoids taking a flyer on attractive stocks just because they fit the growth model. He looks for more of a record and waits until a company gets through adolescence before he gets serious. And if sales, earnings, and his gut tell him the company is overpriced, he's content to sit and wait for a dip before he buys.

Before you label Rogers a strict Graham and Dodd disciple, it's fair to say he does dabble in the world of Peter Lynch and Warren Buffett, which is to say he does watch the broader atmosphere of the economy to the extent that it might change consumers' desire to buy a target company's product. While market fluctuations don't faze him, changing tastes and variations in consumer spending power do.

Plus, he mainly goes for companies that make tangible products, things you can see in everyday life that demonstrate corporate leadership in particular product niches. In other words, Rogers looks for the one widget company that does a better job of making that particular widget than all of its competitors.

"I've really been pushing my research team lately because there are so many broken growth stocks out there," says Rogers. "The small-cap sector is where the value is right now, but it's ending soon. I would figure we're about 80- to 90-percent done with the small-cap correction, so we've moved on some attractive buys."

Rogers is among the most patient of his value brethren: if he loves a stock, it's not uncommon for him to hold the issue for five years. Some of his favorite stocks have been with him for awhile. "We pride ourselves on really getting to know a company over time, not just jumping in for the short haul," he says.

One of his longtime favorites is Specialty Equipment, maker of Taylor ice cream machines (Figure 2-16). It also makes coolers for drink products and dairy products in convenience stores, where it has a majority of the market.

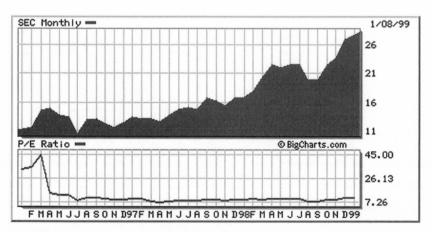

FIGURE 2-16 Specialty Equipment Chart. (*Source:* BigCharts.com)

"It was a stock that had gone through a difficult period and they restructured four years ago. We did our homework and found their two basic markets were very stable and continue to be," said Rogers. "Whatever happens with the economy, I don't think people are going to stop buying soft drinks and ice cream."

In that regard, Rogers holds a similar philosophy to Peter Lynch: He believes in the need for an investor to fully understand the company he or she is investing in.

"I do believe you should invest in things you know or things you actually use if you fully explore the health and prospects for that business," says Rogers. "I think the current market situation has led a lot of people to jump into the market on tips and news, and when you're reading all about a stock, that's usually when it's too late and you're paying too much."

Another "shelf space" investment Rogers's firm has made is Allergan Inc., a company whose primary business used to be contact-lens solution for the medical market, but which now is branching into high-end products to deal with eye disease (Figure 2-17).

"This is a classic Ariel stock in that they've had a couple of bad quarters, they've changed their management, and they're still cheap relative to their peer group," says Rogers. "Some consider them a merger candidate, but that's not a factor we bank on. If anything, we realize our profit sooner if that happens."

In the next chapter, you'll take a closer look at the tools professional and individual investors use to make the kinds of choices listed in this

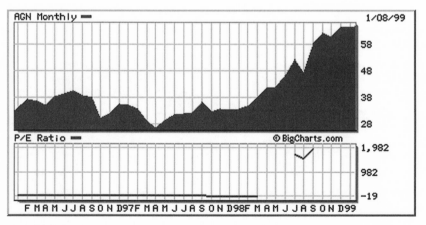

FIGURE 2-17 Allergan Chart. (*Source:* BigCharts.com)

chapter. But it's important to realize that you have the resources that they have; it's all a matter of the time you have to develop a value stock-picking system of your own. In Part 2 and Part 3, you will learn how to put your stock-picking strategy together.

The Value
Investor's Toolbox

CHAPTER 3

Clues to Hidden Value

The Basic Guideposts for Finding Low-Risk Bargain Stocks with Potential

> To be as concrete as possible, let us suggest that an issue is not a true "bargain" unless the indicated value is 50 percent more than the price.[1]
>
> —BENJAMIN GRAHAM

Learning to overcome fear of numbers, particularly the daunting rows and columns of figures that fill the average company's annual report, is the biggest obstacle in determining a company's value. After that, the evidence is in front of you and you're ready to tackle the second-biggest obstacle: seeing if those numbers can support the hunches you've made about the investment you're interested in.

Remember, buying on a hunch without a thorough examination of a company's fundamentals is "speculation," the term Benjamin Graham used derisively to describe investors who don't do their homework. If alive today, Graham would probably get sick of using the word, given the still record-high valuations in the stock market.

In Chapter 2, the investment professionals interviewed made it clear that they are slaves neither to their numbers nor their hunches. Finding value in a business, as Warren Buffett would say, "is part art and part science."[2]

The art comes after you find the facts. This part is all about the science of finding the facts.

However, we can't ignore completely what's going on in today's stock market. Note the technology stock sector. Tech stocks have driven the market to record heights despite balance sheets and income statements that would make Benjamin Graham cringe. We'll explain why some experts believe that value is based as much on great expectations as hard numbers.

Get Ready to Load Up the Toolbox

The next two chapters deal with the basic sources of financial information for a company and the calculations that will help you figure out what all those dollar signs and jargon really mean. Refer to Figure 3-1 for some helpful hints.

While you will see the components of earnings, sales, and asset ratios spelled out for you in detail, the good news is that you won't have to whip out your calculator every time you want to know a specific ratio for an investment you're looking at. Many of these ratios appear in your daily newspaper's stock listings or in the most comprehensive numbers source of all, Value Line publications. And if you're online, you can find these resources and many more with a few keyboard clicks. Those resources will be listed in Chapter 8.

If you're starting to invest, it's a good idea to set up a desk or file cabinet to start organizing these resources. You'll need:

Contents of the Basic Investor's Toolbox

- **Daily newspaper stocks section: For checking prices and popular ratios**
- **Calculator: For figuring out ratios that aren't in the paper**
- **Notebook: Useful for tracking stock gains, losses, and splits if you don't have a computer**
- **File folders: For organizing your research**

Optional, but increasingly useful:

- **Computer with modem: Useful for looking at company web pages, ordering investment information, and tracking stocks online**

FIGURE 3-1 Basic Toolbox List.

Contents of the Basic Investor's Toolbox

- A good business dictionary.
- Business and investing books you've read or want to read (hopefully this one will go there).
- A good tax guide that will help you understand more about your tax situation. This is important because if you learn to save more on your taxes, you'll have more money to save and invest in the future. (Ernst & Young and J. K. Lasser's guides are good, well-organized tax guides with easy-to-find answers. Their cost is also tax deductible.)
- A file cabinet or file box where you can automatically stash news clippings and other reminders on stocks and industries you want to look at. It's also a good place to put personal finance stories on tax issues, commission expenditures, and other financial issues that come up when you invest. You can always start separate file folders on these issues later if you need to. Then you won't be turning the house over later looking for that one piece of information you need.
- A file folder for brokerage statements when you finally open an account to buy stock.

FIGURE 3-1 (continued)

And If You Have a Computer ...

- Consider starting out with an online service like America Online (always best for beginners because of the scope of its content—you can always switch to another, possibly cheaper Internet provider when you learn the ropes). AOL has a good personal finance page or "channel" that allows you to get up-to-the-minute stock prices, investment reports, and key ratios that are explained in this chapter. And its Internet capability allows you to bookmark many of the online resources you'll find in Chapter 8.

Consider buying a budgeting and financial planning software program like Quicken (the market leader) or Microsoft Money. Not that you have to tackle all these things at once, but learning to invest should be only one part of getting your financial act together. As long as you have a computer, it makes sense to have software that can track your spending, taxes, savings, and investments. The real benefit of putting your finances on these programs is forcing yourself to figure out where your money really goes. And once you do that, you can put it to better use.

The Basic Tools for Finding Value

Let's get the nasty stuff over with first. The following formulas and ratios are the key guideposts you'll be looking at when studying a company's balance sheet and income statement (also known as the P&L, or "profit and loss" statement). Further discussion of the importance of the balance sheet and the P&L as well as other key financial statements will come in Chapter 4.

Valuation Ratios

Valuation ratios tell you whether the company is inexpensive or costly on an absolute basis. Your job is to find companies that are bargains relative to their profitability, growth rates, and financial strength. Remember Graham's purchase trigger: If you can find a stock with a value that's 50 percent above the stock price, buy.

1. Price to Earnings Ratio (P/E)

FORMULA

P/E Ratio = Share Price ÷ Earnings Per Share

Where to Find It. P/E is a ratio included next to most individual stock listings in daily papers. Also, you can find annual P/E ratios in Value Line, including comparisons to other stocks in the industry. The main source is the company's income statement.

Why It's Important. If the P/E ratio of a company is less than the industry average P/E, the company is selling at a discount valuation to its peers. When you hear someone refer to a "low P/E," they're referring to an investment that is priced lower than other companies in the industry (also known as its "peer group") and that may be worth a look.

A Warning. Some people think a stock with a 14 P/E is better than buying one with a 40 P/E because the latter company's earnings are so much further below its stock price. (This will be discussed more in Chapter 5.) However, the P/E might be high because those in the know feel the business is expanding quickly enough to create higher earnings at a future point, thus bolstering the company's value. In any event, you must go further to check a company's value. Also, P/E has its own variations. Some investors prefer to use the "12-month trailing" earnings in the denominator of the formula because those are actual earnings. Others like to plug in "forward" earnings estimates. This calculation can get you in trouble if the analysts doing the projecting turn out to be a little too enthusiastic. In Chapter 7, we'll take a closer look at analysts, what they do, and why you should always take what they say with a grain of salt.

2. Price-to-Sales Ratio

FORMULA

P/S Ratio = Current Market Capitalization ÷
Last 12 Months' Total Revenues

Where to Find It. Market capitalization can be found by multiplying the number of shares by the market price. The last four quarters of revenues can be found in Value Line or the last four 10Q statements from the company.

Why It's Important. P/S is a way of valuing companies that aren't earning money or are so young they're practically in the startup phase. In the high-tech sector, many acquisitions are based on P/S because buyers want to know that revenues are headed in an upward trend. If revenues are headed up, good management will control costs and eventually produce earnings. Again, remember that earnings, not sales, ultimately determine a stock's value.

What's a Target Number? P/S aficionados like to see ratios below 1.0.

A Warning. It might make sense to check results against the working capital ratios (following) just to make sure management is using the company's assets the way they should.

3. Book Value

FORMULA

$$\text{Book Value} = \frac{\text{Total Assets} - \text{Intangible Assets} - \text{All Liabilities} - \text{Stock Issues}}{\text{Number of Common Shares Outstanding}}$$

Where to Find It. Book value is listed in the consolidated balance sheet portion of the balance sheet or separately in Value Line. It typically isn't listed in newspapers.

Why It's Important. This is one of the most controversial value ratios because investors like to argue whether the assets posted at their original (or "book" value) could be sold at roughly the same value today. For some industries—banking, for example, which holds a lot of liquid assets on its books, like CDs and Treasury notes and bills—book value may be very accurate to today's value. A business such as a manufacturer with lots of old machinery may have a book value that's too high because its technology is obsolete.

What's a Target Number? If this calculation is below 1.0, then it means that the company is selling below book value—technically below liquidation value. If this is the case, you've either found a gem or a potential problem company, so make sure you study its recent operational history very closely. Some value investors will avoid companies that trade anywhere over 1.5 to 2 times book value.

Generally, though, a low price-to-book-value ratio

$$\frac{\text{Stock Price}}{\text{Book Value}}$$

relative to the rest of that company's competitors is considered a positive sign for investment.

A Warning. Go back to the reasons stated above. It's worth studying the assets the company actually has on its books before you use this signal. A good place to find these observations is in analysts' reports on the company, many of which can be found online or in business news summaries of the company you're researching. However, know the track records of the analysts you're studying. Also, watch out for share buybacks, leveraged buy-outs, and mergers and acquisitions. All three cut book value because assets have to be re-valued as part of closing the deal. And because transactions are singular events, they put the company's price-to-book ratio out of whack.

4. Debt to Equity Ratio

FORMULA

Debt/Equity Ratio = All Current and Noncurrent Liabilities ÷ Total Shareholder's Equity

Where to Find It. You'll find the ratio already figured in Value Line under your chosen company. But if you want to do it yourself, turn to the consolidated balance sheet in the annual report, look for liabilities and shareholders' equity, pick out the numbers, and do the calculation.

Why It's Important. Debt isn't always a bad thing; companies need to borrow on a regular basis to fund short-term needs and long-term expansion. Plus, evidence of speedy repayment makes for a healthy credit rating, just as it does for individuals. This ratio tells you the extent to which the ownership in the company can pay off its debts if the company liquidates.

What's a Target Number? The standard D/E ratio for most companies is 50 percent, meaning investors want $1 of equity for every 50 cents of debt so they won't lose everything in a liquidation. Value investors like to see this number a little lower.

A Warning. Companies take on debt for different reasons. The best reason is for expansion that will generate higher sales and earnings. The worst reason is to keep payroll and other basic expenses covered; that's a company in trouble. Another good way to tell how well a company can manage its debt is to check out its corporate bond rating in Moody's or Standard & Poor's, the leading bond rating services. These ratings may be found in Value Line or the original resources that Moody's and S&P publish. Many libraries carry these. A good rating means you have nothing to worry about; a bad rating means you're taking a chance putting your money in the company. Check the respective services' scale of ratings to understand what's good and what's bad.

5. Profit Margin

FORMULA

Profit Margin = Gross Profit ÷ Total Shares Outstanding

Why It's Important. A higher profit margin (expressed in terms of percentage) with higher sales results each year means a company is controlling costs while growing.

What's a Target Number? The higher the percentage, the better.

6. Net Current Asset Value (also called working capital)

FORMULA

Net Current Asset Value = Current Assets (cash, accounts receivable, inventory) – Current Liabilities

Where to Find It. Go to the current assets and current liabilities section of the consolidated balance sheets in the annual report.

Why It's Important. Working capital is the amount of money a company uses to cover expenses from daily operations, ranging from the price of raw materials to finished goods and sales. Essentially, this measurement shows that a company's assets can pay for its liabilities and is a reflection that management has things under control. It's also a rough measure of liquidating value for a company should it close its doors today.

7. Current Ratio (another way to measure working capital)

FORMULA

Current Ratio = Current Assets ÷ Current Liabilities

Where to Find It. It's always in Value Line, but if you want to figure it out yourself, travel to the same part of the balance sheet where you found the information for debt to equity.

Why It's Important. Again, you want to know that management has assets generating enough capital to fund liabilities.

What's a Target Number? Consensus puts a desirable current ratio at 2, meaning that there is no more than $1 in liabilities for every $2 of assets. A current ratio lower than 2 means that the company is controlling its inventory well and collecting revenues quickly.

8. Quick Ratio

FORMULA

Quick Ratio = Current Assets – Inventory ÷ Current Liabilities

Where to Find It. Go to the same place you looked in the annual report for debt to equity and profit margin. Also check Value Line.

Why It's Important. Say that for some reason, revenues stopped for a period of time. Could the company continue to pay for daily operations until revenues start again?

What's a Target Number? Consensus is that a quick ratio of 1 or lower indicates that a company could meet those obligations.

9. Net Net Asset Value Per Share (the fire-sale ratio)

FORMULA

**Net Net Asset Value Per Share =
Current Assets – Current Liabilities – Long-Term Debt
÷ Total Outstanding Shares**

Where to Find It. All the individual numbers are easily found in Value Line, though you can scrounge the balance sheet to find these too.

Why It's Important. This is actually an arcane formula developed by Benjamin Graham during the Depression when so many companies were hanging by a thread. It was a way to get past the bad news and find out what salable assets actually were there. This is also a formula that investors use to determine the value of companies that have filed for bankruptcy.

What's a Target Number? Graham's target was a stock selling at 33 percent below the net net asset value.

A Warning. Good luck finding stocks fitting Graham's target in this picked-over market. Also, check out the management if you can. This formula can help you find dirt-cheap stocks, but you'd better make sure someone with a brain is in charge for the long haul or that the company might attract a takeover at some point to give you a premium over what you paid.[3]

Other Benchmarks Worth a Look

Dividends

Benjamin Graham was a stickler for dividends, and not just because he was the widows-and-orphans type. He believed a focus on the regular distribution of corporate earnings to shareholders kept management honest. He said:

> It is our belief that stockholders should demand of their managements either a normal payout of earnings—on the order, say, of two-thirds—or else a clearcut demonstration that the reinvested profits have produced a satisfactory increase in per-share earnings. Such a demonstration could ordinarily be made in the case of a recognized growth company. But in many other cases, a low payout is clearly the cause of an average market price that is below fair value, and here the stockholders have every right to inquire and possibly to complain.[4]

Where should the value investor vote, particularly when looking at those tantalizing growth stocks with the high P/Es and stock gains that don't seem to quit? Obviously, he or she should do other calculations that prove there is enough value in the company to watch the stock rise and forego dividends for a while. Graham warns, however, that plowing money back into the business may be good for the business, but it's not good for the shareholders. Simply put, a company that doesn't pay dividends on an annual basis doesn't give shareholders the option of investing those rewards. They lose the benefit of compounding for their own accounts, while the company enjoys it all.

Without dividends, shareholders only see a reward when they sell their stock—assuming it goes up. Graham postulated that shareholders should insist on dividends because it gives them a choice on a quarterly basis of investing those proceeds back in the company or anywhere else they may choose. So keep that in mind when you're thinking about buying into a high-flier that doesn't pay dividends. By the way, you can find out whether a company pays a dividend in some newspaper stock listings, or always in the company's annual report.

Trying an IPO

Buying shares in initial public offerings has been popular in recent years, particularly with the market going sky-high. But results examined by the Chicago-based American Association of Individual Investors show that investment gains are tough to come by, particularly if an investor bypasses a study of assets or previous earnings listed in the prospectus.

> Studies indicate that buying an IPO at the offering price produces above-market risk-adjusted returns, while buying a new offering after it begins trading in the market is more likely to produce negative returns. Unfortunately, these findings are more useful for institutional investors than for individual investors, since most IPOs are offered first to a dealer's largest clients, who quickly snap up the best offers, leaving behind those that are less desirable. If you can get a new offering at the offering price, you probably shouldn't buy it; if you can't get it at the offer price, wait a year or so before you buy it in the secondary market if it still has any appeal.[5]

Intrinsic Value

In all this focus on numbers, there's been little discussion of the value that a company creates based on cultural, brand-name, or other nonfinancial positives that bring in business. Add this value to hard assets that might be undervalued or tough to value in strict monetary terms and you start to get a picture of a company's intrinsic value.

For instance, what is the Starbucks brand name worth? Plenty if you're in a town and don't know where else to go for steaming hot java. Maybe your pair of running shoes wears out on vacation and you go into the nearest department store looking for the Nike "swoosh" symbol. That's intrinsic value, the tough-to-quantify qualities that bring a company business.

Intrinsic value may also involve your belief—hopefully your *well-researched* belief—that this company will develop a profitable following.

There's also plenty of talk about "valuing" corporate knowledge, particularly in high-tech companies where the strength of ideas and concepts (rather than bricks and mortar) are the main assets of the business. It will be interesting if someday someone comes up with a formula to measure that.

CHAPTER

4

Reading Further

Understanding Balance Sheets, Income Statements, and What Management Is *Really* Saying about Operations

> When managers want to get across the facts of the business to you, it can be done within the rules of accounting. Unfortunately, when they want to play games, at least in some industries, it can also be done within the rules of accounting. If you can't recognize the differences, you shouldn't be in the equity-picking business.[1]
> —**WARREN BUFFETT**

If you've ever heard people say annual reports are just window dressing, they're half right. Companies like to make annual reports a showcase for what they do right, not what they do wrong. However, the law requires that all those small gray numbers they put in the back of all those pretty pictures tell the truth about what's really going on.

What we're talking about are the critical numbers contained in the balance sheet, income statement, (also called the earnings statement, or profit and loss [P&L] statement), and various reports on corporate taxes, operational changes, and accounting methods. These are the numbers that will tell you if a stock has value and is truly worth buying.

The purpose of going over all those formulas in Chapter 3 was to provide the tools for picking this data apart. You can get a lot of help from Value Line in crunching the numbers and making sense of them, but you might want to try a few computations just to give yourself the experience. Why?

Most people never feel like investors until they look at their first 401(k) statement or buy their first share of stock. But you'll find that working the numbers is the first step to becoming an *informed* investor, which in the majority of cases will put you ahead of the crowd.

Before we begin the tour of what these components tell you, here's a little more information on sources. This information is found not only in the annual report but also in a company's quarterly financial statements (called 10Qs) and in a plain-text version of the company's glossy annual report that's called the 10K. The Securities and Exchange Commission, the federal government's primary regulatory agency for the markets, gets this 10K report, and you should too.

RESEARCH TIP: WHO'S EDGAR?

Brace yourself: EDGAR is that rare example of your tax dollars being used for something worthwhile. EDGAR is the Electronic Data Gathering, Analysis, and Retrieval system of the Securities and Exchange Commission. Simply put, it's your online connection to every document filed at the SEC. With a few keyboard clicks, you're on the way to finding a wealth of current and historic financial and management data about the stocks, mutual funds, and other securities you're interested in. There's a delay of a day or more if you go to the free SEC site (www.sec.gov), but services like Disclosure allow you to get documents instantly for a charge. In any case, it beats life only a few years ago when the only way to get SEC filings instantly was to pull them off a newswire or go to SEC headquarters in Washington yourself.

The 10K: Not Much Style, but Plenty of Substance

The 10K doesn't have pretty pictures, but it makes up for it with juicy details every investor should know, such as more detailed financials for recent years and even the annual paychecks (and stock options and bonuses) for senior management. Who doesn't like to know what bigshots are earning?

When the company sends you its glossy annual report, it will always include a proxy form that lets you know what issues will be up for a vote at the annual meeting. It's always good to read through the proxy just to make sure your company isn't trying to limit your voting power as a shareholder or do things you don't think the company should be doing.

But companies never include the latest 10K or 10Q. That's mainly because these documents are huge; a typical 10K runs from 35 to 100 pages, single-spaced, depending on what kind of year the company has had. A few years back, you would have had to have someone stationed in Washington at the Securities and Exchange Commission to photo-copy a copy of a 10K and send it to you. Today, you can do the whole process online. Just make sure you have enough paper in your printer. You can find any company's 10K on the Securities and Exchange Com-mission's EDGAR database or a database site that has access to EDGAR. One of the best is Disclosure, where you can get virtually anything you need from the government with the click of a ticker symbol.

For more on what information the major SEC filings can offer investors, see Your Government at Work: How to Make Sense of SEC Fil-ings on page 139.

The Balance Sheet: Your First Stop

Remember the debate mentioned earlier about the usefulness of book value as a measurement of a stock's overall value? Well, debates abound everywhere in the value world. There are some value investors who live by the balance sheet and its focus on total assets, and there are other value investors who look at the income statement and make their deci-sions primarily on what they see in the quality of earnings. As you develop your own method of understanding stocks—and there is no one correct method—you can make up your mind. But it's best to look at both the balance sheet and the income statement for the secrets they reveal.

What Is the Balance Sheet?

Simply defined, the balance sheet reveals the asset value of the company. Your goal in examining the balance sheet is to understand the amount of assets—for that matter, all the figures we're discussing—on a per-share basis so you have an easy and uniform way to compare the amounts from year to year. The balance sheet contains the following components:

- **Assets:** Anything a company could sell for cash if it had to shut the doors and liquidate tomorrow. Assets include cash, accounts receivable (what people owe the company), securities the company invests its cash in to get interest, merchandise in the warehouse and all prepaid expenses, plant and equipment, and "intangibles," i.e., stuff of easily liquidated value that the company doesn't consider as part of the above. As mentioned in the Starbucks example earlier, an intangible could be something like a trademark that another business would like to buy.

- **Liabilities:** What the company owes everyone it does business with. Liabilities include accounts payable (bills for raw materials and other product-related expenses), accrued expenses, and long-term debt (what you would owe lenders if you had to pay them off today). This also includes shareholder equity, the amount of stock, bonds, and notes in shareholders' hands, which represents a stake in the company.

Companies do not necessarily present their balance sheets the same way. They vary in detail. Some provide a "long form," which breaks each element down in its various categories. An abbreviated one summarizes each account. What you'll see most often among established companies is something called the consolidated balance sheet. It combines the assets and liabilities of the parent company with its subsidiary, showing the financial condition of the related companies and the home office as a single unit.

What the Balance Sheet Yields

Of the main ratios and formulas covered in Chapter 3, the balance sheet provides the basic numbers to compute:

- *Debt-to-equity ratio:* The percentage of debt for every $1 of equity; 50 cents or less is generally okay.

- *Working capital:* The amount of money it takes a company to finance its daily obligations. As a per-share amount, investors want to buy stocks priced at two-thirds of this number or less, according to Graham.

- *Current ratio:* Another way to measure working capital. Sound companies have a current ratio of 2 or higher.

- *Quick ratio:* Called the "acid test," this gives a slightly different spin on the everyday strength of the company. The optimal ratio is 1 or higher.

Start Calculating: Walgreen Co.

Before we examine Walgreen Co. balance sheet and income statement for the fiscal year ended Aug. 31, 1997, remember the basic tools. We're going to use the annual report (the glossy one) and our ratios above. First, let's go to a section of the annual report that offers the long-term summary of consolidated financial data. Most companies now list a 10-year summary of all the financial numbers that make up the balance sheet and income statement, and that's a good place to start when trying to get a feel for how the company has progressed— or regressed—over the years. Based on the drug and discount retailer's 1997 annual report, the march in revenues, earnings, and return on shareholder's equity has been steady. Their stock price reflects it (Figure 4-1).

Now for a closer look. Figure 4-2 shows the Walgreens balance sheet.

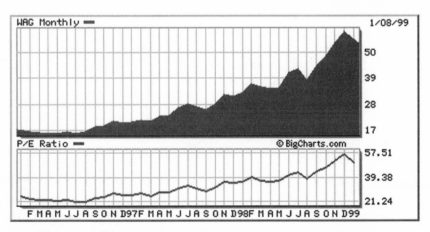

FIGURE 4-1 Walgreens stock chart. (*Source:* BigCharts.com)

Walgreen Co. Balance Sheet Source: 10K Filing (All numbers in $millions)		
Assets		
	1997	1996
Current assets		
Cash and cash equivalents	$ 73	$ 9
Accounts receivable	376	288
Inventories	1,733	1,632
Other current assets	144	90
Total current assets	2,326	2,019
Noncurrent assets		
Property and equipment, at cost, less		
accumulated depreciation and amortization	1,754	1,449
Other noncurrent assets	127	166
Total assets	**$4,207**	**$3,634**
Liabilities and Shareholders' Equity		
Current liabilities		
Trade accounts payable	$ 813	$ 692
Accrued expenses and other liabilities	554	467
Income taxes	72	23
Total current liabilities	1,439	1,182
Noncurrent liabilities		
Deferred income taxes	113	145
Other noncurrent liabilities	282	264
Total noncurrent liabilities	395	409
Shareholders' equity		
Preferred stock, $.125 par value;		
authorized 16 million shares; none issued	—	—
Common stock, $.15625 par value;		
authorized 1.6 billion shares; issued and		
outstanding 493,789,966 in 1997 and		
492,282,144 in 1996	77	77
Paid-in capital	30	——
Retained earnings	2,266	1,966
Total shareholders' equity	2,373	2,043
Total liabilities and shareholders' equity	**$4,207**	**$3,634**

FIGURE 4-2 Walgreens I0K. (Disclosure Source)

What Value Line Says

At mid-year 1998, all forecasts were headed into positive territory for Walgreen Co., the nation's largest drugstore retailer. The company was on target to report record operating results for the end of its fiscal year 1998, which ends August 31. The only negative was Walgreens continued tough negotiations on prescription prices paid by insurers who fund prescription payments for people in their health plans. That's been a fact of life for years for all drugstores, though. Value Line was also predicting higher net income in 1999 as well.

FIGURING DEBT-TO-EQUITY

$$\textit{Remember: Debt-to-Equity Ratio} = \frac{\textit{All Liabilities}}{\textit{Total Shareholders' Equity}}$$

Walgreens Debt-to-Equity Ratio

$$= \frac{1439 \text{ (current liabilities)} + 395 \text{ (noncurrent liabilities)}}{2373 \text{ (total shareholders' equity)}}$$

$$= \frac{1834}{2373} = 0.77$$

This is generally viewed as healthy.

FIGURING WORKING CAPITAL (NET CURRENT ASSET VALUE)

Remember: Working Capital = Current Assets − Current Liabilities

Walgreens Working Capital = 2326 − 1439 = 887*

*Million, which is seen as healthy for the industry it's in.

FIGURING THE CURRENT RATIO

Remember: Current Ratio = Current Assets ÷ Current Liabilities

Walgreens Current Ratio = 2326 ÷ 1439 = 1.61

As mentioned in Chapter 3, a current ratio under 2 is good; it means the company is controlling its inventory and assets well.

FIGURING THE QUICK RATIO

$$\text{Remember: Quick Ratio} = \frac{\text{Current Assets} - \text{Inventory}}{\text{Current Liabilities}}$$

$$\text{Walgreens Quick Ratio} = \frac{2326 - 1733}{1439} = \frac{593}{1439} = 0.41$$

A quick ratio of 1 or under is considered good.

Balance Sheet: Beyond the Ratios

Okay, you have this list of numbers that tells you something. But do you feel you have all you need to know? Maybe not. Here are a few more points to consider when looking at the company's numbers on the balance sheet.

- *Fast inventory turnover.* Having to keep inventory warehoused or stuck on the shelf is an expensive proposition on two fronts. First, you're paying rent to house it. Second, you're losing revenue because it's just sitting there. Here is a standard formula for measuring the time it takes a company to sell its inventory before it has to replace it on the shelves. Use the latest quarterly figures since they're a more up-to-the-minute expression of how quickly inventory is turning. Quarterly figures aren't hard to find if you're online (go to Chapter 10 for a number of websites to find this information). Otherwise, call the company and have them mail or fax the information to you. For more information on why inventory control is such an important issue for investors, turn to Chapter 5. For now check Walgreens 10Q shown in Figure 4-3 and consider its inventory turnover story.

FORMULA

$$\text{Inventory Turnover} = 90 \text{ (the number of days in a quarter)} \div \frac{\text{Revenues}}{\text{Inventory}}$$

$$\text{Walgreens Inventory Turnover} = 90 \div \frac{3887}{1838} = 42.65 \text{ days (as of 5/21/98)}$$

Some might think that the Walgreens inventory turnover doesn't look so hot. Retailers in its peer group typically average a 15- to 20-day turnover of inventory. Walgreens has nearly 43. As year end figures for

Walgreen Co.
Balance Sheet
Source: 10Q ended 5/31/98
(All numbers in $millions, ( ) = loss)

Assets

	5/31/98	5/31/97
Current assets		
Cash and cash equivalents	$ 111	$ 73
Accounts receivable	388	376
Inventories	1,838	1,733
Other current assets	83	144
Total current assets	**2,420**	**2,326**
Noncurrent assets		
Property and equipment, at cost, less accumulated depreciation and amortization of $872 million at May 31 and $748 million at August 31	2,027	1,754
Other noncurrent assets	133	127
Total assets	**$4,580**	**$4,207**

Liabilities & shareholders' equity

Current liabilities		
Trade accounts payable	$795	$813
Other current liabilities	644	626
Total current liabilities	1,439	1,439
Noncurrent liabilities:		
Deferred income taxes	101	113
Other noncurrent liabilities	338	282
Total noncurrent liabilities	439	395
Shareholders' equity:		
Preferred stock $.125 par value; authorized 16 million shares; none issued	—	—
Common stock $.15625 par value; authorized 1.6 billion shares; issued and outstanding 497,147,456 at May 31 and 493,789,966 at August 31	78	77
Paid-in capital	93	30
Retained earnings	2,531	2,266
Total shareholders' equity	2,702	2,373
Total liabilities & shareholders equity	**$4,580**	**$4,207**

FIGURE 4-3 Walgreens 10Q 5/31/98. (Disclosure Source)

	5/31/98	5/31/97
Walgreen Co. Income Statement Source: 10Q ended 5/31/98 (All numbers in $millions, ( ) = loss)		
Net sales	$ 3,887	$3,403
Costs and deductions:		
Cost of sales	2,840	2,470
Selling, occupancy, and administration	843	758
Other (income) expense:		
Interest income	(2)	(2)
Interest expense	1	1
Earnings before income tax provision and cumulative effect of accounting change	206	176
Income tax provision	79	68
Earnings before cumulative effect of accounting change	127	108
Net earnings	**$ 127**	**$ 108**
Per share	**$ 0.25**	**$ 0.21**
Dividends declared	$0.0625	$0.0600
Average shares outstanding	497	492
Dilutive effect of stock options	7	6
Average shares outstanding assuming dilution	504	498

FIGURE 4-3 (*Continued*)

1998 come out, it will be interesting to do that computation and read further about business conditions that affected inventory and what the company is doing about it.

- *Plenty of cash on the balance sheet.* In Walgreens case, there's plenty of cash—$73 million in 1997 compared to $9 million in 1996. Cash-rich companies don't have trouble funding growth or paying their bills.

- *Small amount of long-term debt.* Walgreens has virtually no long-term debt, based on the 1997 report. For a $13 billion company, having $3 million in long-term debt indicates that most of the expansion is being done through money generated by operations, which indicates a very healthy company.

- *Low accounts receivable.* It's great to have money coming to you, but unless a company is charging daily interest on every one of its invoices (like credit card companies do), the company is essentially lending out money for free. Unfortunately, this is what companies do for their clients. So here is another formula that will help you track the average number of days it takes a company to collect its receivables. Again, use the quarterly numbers.

FORMULA

$$\text{Days to Collect Receivables} = 90 \div \frac{Revenues}{Accounts\ Receivable}$$

$$\text{Walgreens Days to Collect Receivables} = 90 \div \frac{3887}{388} = 90 \div 10$$

$$= \textbf{9 Days to Collect Receivables}$$

Typically, companies allow 30 days before charging interest or additional fees to those owing them money. Here, Walgreens looks very good. It looks like the men and women of this company's collections department deserve a hand—or a bonus!

- *High accounts payable.* When is it good to have bills stacking up at a company? When you don't have to pay interest on them. This is essentially the reverse of the receivables rule. However, just because Walgreens gets paid in nine days doesn't mean that it can wait 90 days to pay its own bills. First, it's expensive if its creditors are charging interest past 30 days. Second, it's not a good business practice. People won't want to deal with a company if they're not paid in a timely way. They can find other companies to deal with.

- *Good cash flow.* We haven't talked much about cash flow in this book, but here's a good formula and some explanation of how important cash flow is to a business.

Cash Flow and the Precious Few Who Understand It

Sure, we all know what cash flow is. Open your wallet. No cash in there? You don't have poor cash flow, you have *no* cash flow.

Actually, there's a bit more to it than that.

Some investors go their whole lives without understanding cash flow. Heaven knows, you read about enough failing businesses managing to

Cash Flow and the Precious Few Who Understand It (*Continued*)

do the same thing. But this is important stuff, key to a company's survival, and on a personal level, key to your kids' education, your retirement fund, your stash for vacations, and so on. You get the picture. So it's good to grasp the concept before starting working the numbers.

Why is cash flow important? It helps to understand the concept a little better if you think about your own financial situation. Think of cash flow as cash in your hand—or in your checking account—after all your regular bills are paid for the month. Cash flow is the amount of *real* money you, a company, or anyone still has after paying for raw materials, salaries—all the stuff necessary to run a household or a business.

Money left over after you pay all the bills: Isn't that profit? Good question; now you get to understand why so many people don't trust number-crunchers. Cash flow is one of those great elusive concepts where accountants, executives, and ordinary folks like to use their own definition, the one that makes *their* numbers look the best. Before going into a three-book series on all the weird junk bean-counters can stuff into their definitions of cash flow, here's why cash flow isn't profit.

Let's look at your checking account again. Say you paid all the bills last week and you had $78 left over for emergencies, savings, or investment (which would be reinvestment in yourself, by the way, and therefore a very good idea). Then, three weeks later, you get your regular paycheck and the same monthly bills. But your credit card bill's a little higher and your monthly auto premium went up. After you seal the last envelope, you find you have a whopping $15 left over. This is an example of your daily cash flow at two different points in time—snapshots actually.

And this is the whole point. Cash flow, in its simplest form, is *cash left over at any specified point in time* after all your obligations and bills are paid. Profit, for a company, is the amount of daily operating cash and other sources of funds (like investment income or the sale of assets) collected at the end of a specified term (the end of a quarter or year, usually) that can be reinvested in a business or paid out in dividends.

People look at cash flow to determine whether a business has money in the kitty at the end of the day to take care of any emergency needs that come up. Investors like to see that, because borrowing to fix a problem costs money. Profit is what you have at the end of a reporting period that allows you to reinvest in the business or pay out to your shareholders.

Cash flow is part of a company's profit, but it isn't profit itself.

Let's get back to our calculators.

Here's a useful formula to determine whether cash flow is adequate or inadequate for a company's needs. There are different variations on this, but this is the most widely used formula to determine cash flow.

FORMULA

$$Cash\ Flow = \frac{Current\ Assets - Cash\ (and\ equivalents)}{Current\ Liabilities}$$

Walgreens Cash Flow (using 5/31/98 quarterly figures)

$$= \frac{2420 - 111}{1439} = 1.60$$

For its peer group, some would think Walgreens cash flow is below par, since its target ratio is 1.25 or below.

What the Income Statement Yields

Figure 4-4 illustrates a typical income statement, in this case, one from Walgreens.

Walgreen Co. Income Statement Source: 10K Filing (All numbers in $millions)		
	1997	1996
Revenues	$13,363	$11,778
Costs and deductions		
Cost of sales	9,682	8,515
Selling, occupancy and administration	2,973	2,659
Net revenues	12,655	11,174
Other (income) expense		
Interest income	(6)	(5)
Interest expense	2	2
Earnings		
Earnings before income tax provision	712	607
Income tax provision	276	235
Net earnings	**$436**	**$372**
Net earnings per common share	**$0.88**	**$0.75**

FIGURE 4-4 Walgreens 10K. (Disclosure Source)

Following assets, earnings is the other sacred measuring stick for the value investor. What a company earns is important not just for the dollar figure or for the fact that it earned something but for the way management treats those earnings.

Benjamin Graham came up with his own laundry list of what makes a stock's earnings-related features worth looking at.[2]

- *Earnings stability:* Some earnings for common stock in each of the past 10 years measured annually.

- *Earnings growth:* A minimum increase of at least one-third in per-share earnings in the past 10 years at the beginning and end.

- *Price-to-earnings ratio:* Current price should not be more than 15 times average earnings of the past three years.

- *Dividend payouts:* Uninterrupted payments for the last 20 years.

One might say Graham wasn't a Microsoft kind of guy—and *certainly* not an Amazon.com kind of guy! His very conservative theories of investing would probably lead many investors who have locked-in profit on some of the most high-flying tech stocks of today to scoff at the low P/E ratios he targeted. The man insisted on regular dividends for *20 years,* for Pete's sake! Microsoft, one of the stock darlings of the modern age, has *never* paid a dividend. One might be curious to hear what Graham would say about today's market, though student Warren Buffett has his own commentary on the market in general: "Happily, there's more than one way to get to financial heaven."

So here are some of the tools to be extracted from the income statement.

Price-to-Earnings Ratio

The P/E is the most familiar ratio to average investors because it's the easiest to find; your local newspaper will run it every day. To review, it is the current price of the stock divided by the past four quarters' earnings per share. Example: A company with earnings per share of $3 is selling at $15. It is selling at five times earnings. This is known as the *trailing P/E* because you've figured it on past earnings. *Leading P/E* is based on future estimates of earnings, usually left to analysts. Don't buy a stock based on P/E alone, though. It's a good way to start looking at a stock, but not the only one.

RESEARCH TIP

What's an attractive P/E? One investor's favorable P/E is another's signal to run away. But like all of the ratios and formulas listed in this book, everything is subject to interpretation and your tolerance for risk. Actually, Graham recommended that to find a true bargain, you should look at stocks with P/Es under 15 for the last three years as a *starting point* for finding a bargain. Not that below-15 P/E stocks are impossible to locate, but in the galloping market of the last decade, it's sure been tough to find a lot of quality at that level. However, here are some good guidelines when you look at P/E:

- Is your chosen company's P/E lower than other stocks in its peer group (competitors who serve similar markets)?

- If so, return to your balance sheet calculations, review to see if there were any trouble spots that might account for the low multiple, and build your case from there.

Many of the most talked-about stocks of the decade have P/Es of 30 or more—Microsoft, Intel, and similar growth stocks among them. Many investors ignore high P/Es because they are confident the underlying plans for corporate growth will bolster the value of a stock.

The Microsoft chart (Figure 4-5) shows that shareholders have benefited tremendously in terms of stock price and number of shares (note the splits), even though Microsoft doesn't pay dividends and has a P/E these days over 40. Again, as the investor, it's your call.

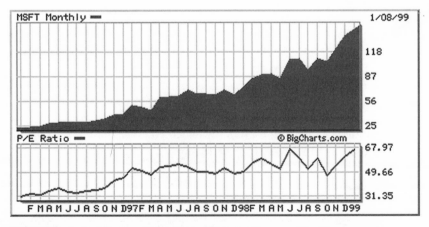

FIGURE 4-5 Microsoft 10-Year Chart. (*Source:* BigCharts.com)

WALGREEN CO.'S P/E RATIO

The simplest way to check Walgreen Co.'s current P/E would be to open the business section of your local newspaper. But since we want to run the exercise, we're going to use the company's latest stock price as of late September 1998, with the latest earnings per share reported at that time. Of course, for historic P/Es, you may want to pick up your company's listing in Value Line.

FORMULA

Remember: P/E = Current Stock Price ÷ Annual Earnings per Share (EPS)

Walgreens P/E = \$47 ÷ 0.99 (EPS) = 47 Times Earnings, or 47

Perhaps Benjamin Graham would have stayed away from this stock based on P/E alone, but look at the other factors:

1. The company has paid dividends every quarter since 1933 and raised them in each of the last 21 years.

2. Its market capitalization (the total dollar value of all securities issued by a company) grew by \$5 billion in 1997 to a total of \$13 billion.

3. Earnings and revenues have increased without fail during the last 10 years.

4. The company has almost no debt and very healthy working capital ratios.

Okay, Graham might not dismiss it outright. But he'd probably wait for a market tumble to drive the price down a bit. Of course, he probably would have been smart enough to buy Walgreens in 1933.

Profit Margin

Profit margin is a good figure to know when you're watching a company in a very competitive industry like retailing.

FORMULA

$$\text{Profit Margin} = \frac{\textit{Gross Profit (earnings before taxes and other charges)}}{\textit{Total Outstanding Shares}}$$

$$\text{Walgreens Profit Margin} = \frac{206m}{494m} = 41.7\%$$

Revenues

Revenues, often referred to as "the top line" in the income statement (because it is the first line of figures on the statement) are very important; if you don't sell anything, you can't pay your bills, and there won't be anything left over as earnings. Again, there are some general ideas about revenue growth that investors use to make a stock purchase:

- *Annual revenue growth of 8 to 15 percent is ideal.* Older companies with $5 billion in sales or more (like Walgreens) are perfect for this definition, but companies smaller than this should have a recent record of 20 to 30 percent a year, since they're in growth mode. Walgreens revenues were up 13 percent in 1997 from year-ago levels, so its obviously meeting this criteria.

- *Cost of sales shouldn't be growing faster than revenues.* At Walgreens, sales were up 13 percent for the year, so that's the limit for the cost-of-sales measurement. The company's income statement said cost of sales was $9.7 billion in 1997. That's a 14-percent increase over 1996. This percentage doesn't indicate any serious problems, but the bean-counters need to watch costs a little more closely at Walgreens as a result.

- *High gross margin is nice.* We're not talking about profits here. When you see "gross," it's generally referring to numbers closer to revenues, not net income. Retailers like to see this figure around 30 to 40 percent. Here's how to get the figure for Walgreens:

FORMULA

Gross Margin = Gross Profit (earnings before deductions) ÷ Total Revenues

$$\text{Walgreens Gross Margin} = \frac{12,655}{13,363} = 94\%$$

This is a very good figure.

Rising R&D Costs

Walgreens isn't in the business of manufacturing microprocessors, but research and development (R&D) for a retailer may mean better ways to sell something. In the Walgreens case, R&D spending in 1997 went toward building more drive-through prescription windows to service customers on the go and installing software to help people phone in prescription refills. It's not inventing a new microchip, but any investment directed at boosting sales pretty much falls into this category, so watch for it. Also, make sure, when you're reading about the company's past performance, to see if any of these investments were clunkers and why.

A 34-Percent Tax Rate

Some believe that paying the max to Uncle Sam is usually a good sign for a company, since it means the company hasn't diluted its earnings growth from tax losses carried forward. For this figure, it's best to go straight to Value Line because Walgreens and other companies tend to express their tax payments in dollar figures instead of percentages of earnings. You can do the math, but in this case it's not worth the time. According to Value Line, Walgreens paid 38.8 percent of its income in taxes in 1997, so it's on target.

RESEARCH TIP: WATCH THOSE TAXES

When you're looking at a company's results over the years, see if there is any mention of tax troubles and how they were solved. Obviously, if a company is paying more taxes because of an accounting snafu, see if its hired better bean-counters afterward (many analysts' reports tell these stories quite well). If its paying less than the corporate tax rate of 34 percent, find out why and see how it's impacted the earnings you're buying.

In the next chapter, we'll take a look at how you should actually go about buying these stocks you've carefully researched, and how to avoid putting too many of the same eggs in one basket.

CHAPTER 5

Inventory Turnover

And other Spine-Tingling Secrets to Better Investing

A whole chapter devoted to inventory. Start the coffee. Stay with us, though. There is a very good reason to talk about this less-than-exciting subject.

For instance, did you know that next to payroll and benefits, managing and warehousing inventory is one of the highest costs of running a business? And did you know that if left uncontrolled, inventory costs can create one of the biggest drags on the value of your stock?

Today, many businesses are taking a hard look at how they manage their inventories, and it's redefining the way they run their whole operation. This is a book about value investing, but finding out how inventory works within a company may be one of the best ways to determine how the business is being run overall. And well-run businesses are able to create lots of value for their shareholders.

Goldman, Sachs & Co. market analyst Abby Joseph Cohen has an interesting theory about inventory and the economy. "In the 1970s, whatever you bought at the supermarket on the last trip was always a few cents higher on the next trip," she says. "So you bought two to beat the next increase. Businesses did the same and built excess inventory, figuring they could sell it for more later."

Her point is that such behavior fed inflation. Now that inflation has abated in the 1990s, consumers have also adopted a behavior of waiting for sales and lower prices to buy what they need. We're now in something of a value culture. Businesses, if they want to stay in business, have responded by keeping inventories as tight as possible. This means having enough merchandise available to supply consumers' immediate needs.

Whether or not you agree with Cohen's theory of how businesses and consumers changed their behavior from the 1970s to the 1990s, you've already heard about the importance of keeping inventories as lean as possible. Think about it. You're in business and you make things. You decide how to make these things based on your theory of how many things your customers will need and when they'll need them.

Well, what if your theory is wrong? Then you're stuck with a warehouse full of things that you need to sell so you can pay your employees, your creditors, and your landlord for the warehouse space you keep all those things in. To get rid of those things, you cut prices, which means you cut revenue, and eventually, after you pay all the bills, you have fewer earnings to pay your shareholders in dividends or to plow back into the business.

That's a very simplistic view of the bad things that happen when you have too much inventory. The truth is that inventory can represent either good or bad in a business, and the investor's job is to recognize when the balance is a good one. In accounting terms, inventory is totaled as part of a firm's assets; it's something you can sell to bring in dollars. Yet inventory can become a liability if it is a drain on the earning power of a business.

Let's go back to the simplistic example. Remember how we used the word *theory* to describe how the business handled its inventory? Well, for years many businesses believed that the best way to stay in business was to have enough inventory to cover any eventuality. Before the sophistication of personal computers and Internet technology changed record-keeping at businesses large and small, companies mainly would predict future results on past behavior—and deal with the realities later.

Today, technology is changing not only the way businesses treat inventory but also the way they create that inventory, all the way back to the design phase. They've done it by using customer orders—rather than customer expectations—as the trigger for building inventory.

Dell's Example

One of the hottest technology stocks in the marketplace is Dell Computer, the build-to-order computer manufacturer based in Austin, Texas. It's not surprising that a computer company has figured out the best way to make use of computer, phone, and Internet technology to create inventory the minute a customer orders it.

At Dell Computer's main assembly facility near Austin, supplier trucks full of microprocessors and various hardware and software components roll up to Dell's loading docks with choreographed precision.

A few hours earlier, those trucks were loaded and launched by a keyboard stroke that originated from a Dell customer who was ordering a new laptop computer online. With that online order transmitted within seconds to Dell's sales department, the information then traveled at light speed to Dell's supplier base, to their factory floors, and back to the suppliers' logistics departments, letting Dell know when the necessary components would arrive at Dell's assembly point for final construction and delivery to the customer.

And if all goes smoothly—as it usually does—that Dell customer's computer order will ship by day's end, which is why Dell's average inventory rate of seven to eight days is the envy of the computer industry.

"Most of our competitors want to get to 20 days; we know that most of them average between 60 and 90 days in turning inventory," notes T.R. Reid, spokesman for Dell Computer. "As the Internet evolves, we will eventually be talking hours rather than days."

That's a very important point. As more companies learn how to change the focus of creating inventory from the plant floor to the consumer who orders it, inventory turnover is bound to get shorter. Dell's example holds lessons for all industries able to link their customer communication, marketing, supplier, manufacturing, and inventory management functions through a single electronic path.

"Really, what's happening here is that the whole problem of inventory is being moved to the customer," says Jay Collins, a senior manager at Chicago-based Arthur Andersen, who deals with cost-management issues at companies. "If it's done right, e-commerce allows the customer to make the first move that affects the whole inventory management process going back to the manufacturer. That means your inventory is always tied to the real needs of your customer, not some projection you've made that might be right or wrong."

High inventories, besides raising operating costs, present a particular evil to Dell, spokesman Reid explains. "We find that standing inventory both creates and hides quality problems. You're moving stuff around, you're warehousing it, it goes through more hands, and you find you have a greater possibility of breakage or defects. If you are able to move a device quickly to its end user, you can focus on eliminating those defects on the factory floor and immediately get it into the hands of the person who wants it."

What to Watch For

Keep an eye on inventory turnover. Remember, that formula is

$$\text{Inventory Turnover} = \frac{\textbf{90 (the number of days in the average quarter)}}{\textbf{Revenues/Inventory}}$$

Also, remember to keep track of any news the company provides on ways it is streamlining its inventory processes. Changing an inventory system is typically an expensive proposition, so the company will have to list the progress of the effort in its results. The annual report and 10K will probably have the most detail.

When to Buy

Creating a Diverse Portfolio Using Value Principles

> The "aggressive" investor should start from the same base as the defensive investor, namely, a division of his funds between high-grade bonds and high-grade common stocks bought at reasonable prices....Let him leave high-grade preferred stocks to corporate buyers. Let him also avoid inferior types of bonds and preferred stocks unless they can be bought at bargain levels— which means ordinarily at prices at least 30 percent under par for high coupon issues, and much less for the lower coupons.[1]
>
> **—BENJAMIN GRAHAM**

In other words, diversify. In the last few years, the number of dollars going into mutual funds began exceeding the amount going into individual company stocks.

So you might wonder: Why have I just gone through the headaches of picking stocks individually in the last four chapters when I can just find somebody to do all the number-crunching for me?

Well, that's an option. Investment in mutual funds has been, by and large, the fastest-growing investment option over the last 10 years (see Figure 6-1). That's because mutual funds offer a full range of options in stocks, bonds, and money markets, much the same options individual investors have historically gone after on their own.

But the principles you've just learned apply to any type of investment. Above all, you are looking for financially healthy investments selling at a

Funds Are King			
Statistics show most American investors, both small and institutional, have chosen to go the mutual fund route with their investment dollars. The combined assets of the nation's mutual funds stood at $5.158 trillion as of July 1998 according to the Investment Company Institute, the leading trade organization for the mutual fund industry.			
Here is how the assets of the six major fund categories changed during that month. (Net assets of mutual funds, in billions of dollars)			
	July 1998	June 1998	Change (%)	June 1997
Stock funds	2,814.1	2,844.5^R	21.1	2,272.8
Hybrid funds	356.3	357.4^R	20.3	305.0
Taxable bond funds	508.7	502.9^R	11.1	421.7
Municipal bond funds	283.2	282.1^R	10.4	262.6
Taxable money market funds	1,015.6	995.2^R	12.1	833.5
Tax-free money market funds	180.5	173.3^R	14.2	152.1
Total	5,158.4	5,155.5^R	10.1	4,247.6

^{R} = revised data

FIGURE 6-1 Mutual Fund Trend Chart. (*Source:* Investment Company Institute, Washington, D.C.)

discount against their peers. And most investment experts would encourage you to put your investment dollars in a variety of areas, not just stocks.

David Katz, portfolio manager for the Matrix/LMX fund, says that mutual fund managers can apply value principles to many more stocks than the average investor can, which is the advantage of owning mutual funds. But he and other investment professionals interviewed for this book say that an investor who puts money in the hands of others without understanding the basic principles of investing are "cheating themselves out of an education."

"No question, fund managers perform an important function in our market economy because so many of us are helping people invest," says Katz. "But I don't think any of us feel that investors need to abdicate their education about investing as a result. If you don't understand what you're buying, why are you buying it?"[2]

John Rogers of Ariel Capital concurs: "I think the main difference between professionals like ourselves and the individual investor is resources and training. Resources—databases and so on—can be a big issue, but training is something available to everyone. And when you consider the amount of free information online and in bookstores and in the media, there's no reason why people can't learn how to buy good companies at low multiples that will grow."[3]

Creating a Portfolio—Some Basic Steps

Is there any one correct way to create a portfolio? Of course not. Do you suddenly need to go out and buy five, ten, or thirty stocks at once so you have a portfolio? Definitely not. A portfolio is a collection of investments—and not just stocks—that can be relied upon to keep their value while blunting losses of other types of investments you own.

In other words, you're trying to achieve balance in your investments so when one goes down, you have others that will stay up and hopefully gain ground.

Graham made his statement at the top of this chapter before the explosion of mutual funds for individual investors, but the reasoning is clear. You shouldn't buy only one class of investments, and whatever you buy you should buy at a discount to its peer group—once you've checked the fundamentals.

Other Points to Follow

- *Know what you want to accomplish.* Very few people sit down and ask themselves exactly what they want to do with their money. Most will say "retire" or "send my kids to college" and leave it at that. But *how* do you want to spend retirement? If you're thirty now, do you plan to retire at fifty or seventy? And then, do you want to keep working part-time? Is your kid likely to go to state school for four years, or add medical school for another six to ten years? Creating a successful investment portfolio doesn't mean just making a lot of money. It also means understanding what that money will be used for.

- *Diversify.* One of the best ways to do this is to seek a balance between your age, the amount of risk you can tolerate, and the length of time until you need to cash in your investments. And don't simply pick categories of stocks, bonds, and funds and let them sit there. Most investment professionals say to set clear percentages of money you plan to invest and to check those investments regularly. They call this a *fixed-weight strategy* and recommend you reevaluate it at least once a year. When stocks rise from being fairly valued to overvalued (something that will be discussed further in Chapter 8), you sell from the overvalued stock holdings and buy more bonds (or set aside cash). Or when you put more money into your portfolio, you can buy bonds or money market investments rather than stocks. When stocks fall from being fairly valued to undervalued, you sell bonds and buy the undervalued stocks, or you use new money to buy stocks. To do this efficiently and safely, you have to keep an eye on things.

- *Diversify more; understand the relationship between stocks and bonds.* Stocks are claims against real assets. Bonds and cash are debt, usually promising fixed returns. All you need to understand is that stock and debt are fundamentally different animals. Consequently, their returns tend not to follow similar patterns. Therefore, combining stocks and debt moderates a portfolio's risk. On a broader scale, individuals who hold stocks and debt in their investment portfolios and own their own homes have their broad portfolio diversified among stocks, debt, and real estate, three asset types whose returns do not track closely together.

- *Forget about market timing.* Market timing essentially means you try to predict what the market is going to do based on certain indicators and then invest accordingly. This isn't the way value investors act. In fact, Warren Buffett has gone on record many times saying he doesn't care what the overall market does, since his tests for individual investments ensure they are safe in any market or any economy.

- *Double-check your birth certificate.* The longer you have until retirement, the larger the portion of your portfolio that should be allocated to stocks. Young investors who are years from retirement can invest more of their portfolios in stocks than the elderly. Although year-to-year stock returns can be volatile, the young can be reasonably confident that the good years will more than offset the bad years over their investment horizon. As you age and your investment horizon shortens, you are less confident that there will be enough good years to offset the bad, and the recommended allocation to stocks decreases. Usually before investors need to tap assets, they downshift from volatile investments like stocks to more stable fixed investments like CDs and Treasury bills. If safeguarding principal and return is your priority, moving slowly—and not completely—into the fixed-income area is the way to go.

- *You may be old, but you're not dead yet.* Everyone should have some exposure in stocks, even people in their eighties and beyond. Statistics show that a portfolio of long-term Treasury bonds has been more volatile (that is, riskier) than a portfolio with 90 percent bonds and 10 percent common stocks. Holding only stocks is riskier than holding only bonds, but due to the magic of diversification, you can add some stock to an all-bond portfolio and actually reduce the portfolio's risk. Since 1926, the volatility of an 80-percent bond/20-percent stock portfolio has been equal to that of a 100% bond portfolio. This helps explain why no one recommends a stock weight of less than 20 percent.

As you age, shift the bond portion of the portfolio from primarily long-term bonds to primarily intermediate-term or short-term bonds. Bond prices become more stable as maturity shortens. Thus the advice to shorten bond maturity as you age is consistent with the other advice to move toward assets with more stable prices. Also, as you age, the cash portion of the portfolio should increase. Increasing cash assets is part of shortening the bond maturity for increased price stability. High-grade corporate bonds and Treasury bonds of similar maturity are close substitutes.

- *Diversify even more—within categories of investments.* Value investors like bargains with conservative fundamentals, but you should also entertain younger stocks if your research shows that their earnings will grow quickly. The latter tend to have low dividend yields, high price-earnings ratios, and high price-to-book-value ratios. Diversification within a stock portfolio would consist of investing some portion in each of these areas—large- and small-capitalization stocks (with proportions roughly equal to their weighting in the total stock market, about a 75/25 percent large-cap/small-cap mix), and growth and value stocks.

- *Going international is fine; just know where you're going.*   Established international firms that trade on U.S. exchanges in the form of American depositary receipts (ADRs) typically also have analyst coverage. Therefore, if you are familiar with an overseas company that seems to have prospects in the U.S. and abroad, you should research it with an eye toward possible purchase. Despite the problems in emerging markets, there are stable economies and companies the world around, and investing in them is another way you can diversify.

RESEARCH TIP: HOW TO GET IDEAS ON INTERNATIONAL INVESTMENTS

The first rule of investing is to never put your money in things you don't understand. But if you want to educate yourself on the type of stocks talented investors put their money in, take a look at the best-performing international funds that may be listed in leading personal finance publications. Then get a prospectus for some of these funds—some are online—and find out the top ten investments those funds are involved in. If any interest you as individual stocks, do your homework and see if they may be worth the investment.

Ways to Invest

There is no rule that says anyone building a portfolio needs to start with $10,000 or more. Some people hold off investing because they only have a couple hundred dollars left over each month and they believe that they can't put together a respectable nut to get started. Not true. You can start investing at any time, and the earlier in your life, the better.

This is why so many investors get started with mutual funds, with their low entry costs and the security of someone with a proven five-to-ten-year track record managing your money. Some mutual funds will allow investors to open accounts with initial deposits of $250 or less. But if you are going to be a true value investor, don't think only about the gains you'll be making in the market. Make sure your costs associated with managing your investments are kept to a minimum. So here are some things you should think about.

Mutual Fund Fees

Try to invest in no-load funds and funds that keep fees to a minimum. *No-load funds* are funds that don't charge a sales fee, but some funds charge up to 1 percent and call themselves no-load, so watch it. The *12b-1 fee,* named after its placement in the tax code, is an annual fee that's supposed to be used for marketing and administrative expenses. Sometimes, though, funds that close themselves to new investors keep charging these fees—when they have nothing to market. Also, a fund family that charges more than 0.25 percent of the total investment in 12b-1 fees cannot advertise itself as no-load, so ask about that before you invest. If your fund has a load, it is usually a *front-end load* (charged when you buy), or *back end load* (charged when you sell).

Other people start their portfolios with ownership in one or more companies purchased through shares of stock. As we mentioned before, some people think it's good to start with $5000 or $10,000, and that's great, because you can buy more of what you want. Others say you should buy no less than 100 shares of a company your first time out—anything less is known as an *odd lot.* Actually, the 100-share point has slightly more credence, since small purchases of shares tend to complicate bookkeeping when you sell.

Some basic bookkeeping advice for starting a portfolio:

- *Compare brokers.* Whether you are going online or with a full-service broker you contact in person or by phone, never hesitate to check their pricing of trades based on the amount of stock you want to buy. Also, decide whether you want access to brokerage research or are willing to do your own research. Full-service brokers—particularly the largest, like Merrill Lynch and Shearson—have extensive research teams that produce investment information on various companies for their clients. However, much of this information is disseminated on the Internet after it's published.

- *Start an investment filing system.* Granted, value investors are buy-and-hold types, which means it may be years before you decide to sell a stake in a portfolio you've built. This is all the more reason to set up a reliable filing and record-keeping system for all your investments. For tax purposes, you will want to record every transaction based on share price, the amount of shares purchased, and the commissions and any other fees assessed to that trade and your account. When you sell a stock, the IRS will ask you for the basis price of your investment, in other words, the pure purchase value of your investment less commissions and fees. That's why putting a date with every transaction, commission, and fee assessment *is essential*. The shoebox method of organization is fine for some folks, but if you're computerized, many investment programs like Quicken and Microsoft Money provide ready-made record-keeping systems that ask you all the right questions. Of course, you can also create your own file and documents by hand.

RESEARCH TIP: PLANNING FOR THE INEVITABLE

Who thinks about dying or becoming permanently incapacitated when they're thirty or forty? Well, if you've had the foresight to buy life insurance or make a will while you're young, you should at least devote equal time to organizing your finances in a way to make a painful time easier for your heirs. This isn't a book about estate planning, but if you're starting a portfolio, it makes sense to organize your investment record-keeping system with an eye toward quick access for your executor or person with power of attorney to find your assets if you die or become incapacitated. Consult your estate attorney or your financial advisor on this issue. They may have some really good suggestions for your situation. There's one good habit to get into: Each year, at the time you review your investments, create a one-page index of your holdings, with dollar amounts, purchase dates, account numbers, and brokers. This will enable a trusted friend or family member to find this information quickly and begin the process of using your assets to fund your care or settling your estate for your heirs.

Now that you've started to organize your investment strategy, the next chapter tells you a little about the pundits and experts who assail you with information.

Call Me a Pundit.
Okay, You're a Pundit!
Knowing Who's an Expert and Who Isn't

There was a time when investment information, good investment information at least, was available only to those with money to begin with.

Today, that's all changed, and mainly for the better.

Solid investment information—for individuals practicing value investing or other disciplines—is available in volumes never before seen in our society. Whole TV networks are devoted to coverage of business and the markets. The Internet has spawned thousands of useful—and not so useful—sites, and print media has exploded on the subjects of investment and personal finance.

But how do you find experts you can trust? This chapter deals with ways to judge the quality of information you read, hear, and click to. Hopefully, you'll depart with one important piece of knowledge: No one is right or wrong 100 percent of the time.

A Few Words about Crooks...

Let's start with the lowest common denominators in investment information. The con men, and women, who deliberately sucker ignorant investors into "can't miss" investment opportunities that end up missing big time. You—and most people reading this book—are smart enough to avoid these scams. If you're willing to turn a skeptical eye toward any investment information, including what you're reading right now, you'll probably be able to avoid the hucksters who steal, according to the Federal Trade Commission, over $100 million a year in investors' dollars.

Their scams actually don't go that far into stocks, since the stock and mutual funds markets are relatively well regulated. They play more in the world of so-called rare coins, precious metal scams, and fake limited partnership deals and pyramid schemes. They connect through the Internet and through telemarketing boileroom operations.

...And Those Not Bright Enough to Be Crooks

As much as the Internet has helped spread a wealth of useful information about investing, it has also freed a lot of people to babble about any half-baked investment theory or hot tip they have. We're talking primarily about the Internet chatroom phenomenon, where individuals of like minds gather to talk about anything from collecting Hummels to trading stock. Chatrooms operate with a sea of faceless, nameless personalities exchanging information that can be right or wrong, afloat because members often believe that insiders at various companies log on and share insider information, which is illegal, by the way. The Securities and Exchange Commission takes a dim view of individuals and company insiders who profit on key corporate information that has not been released to the public.

The Right Way to Look for Clues to Value

Yes, hot tips abound. Some of them work, spiking the prices of certain stocks into rarified territory that makes buyers look like geniuses. But more often than not, hot tips fizzle, either because the information was flawed or because the last investors got in just as the smart ones were getting out.

As we've stressed in previous chapters, true value is found by piecing together a puzzle of conclusions based on simple, accurate information that's already available to the public at large. In addition to numbers, there are news reports that disseminate timely, accurate information about businesses as developments happen. News of big orders, new partnerships, mergers, acquisitions, advances in technology: these are all parts of the landscape that people should consider when evaluating an investment.

Who Are All These Analysts Anyway?

If you read your daily newspaper's business section or national newspapers like *The Wall Street Journal,* you'll notice several types of experts quoted in stories:

- *Company officials:* Optimally, reporters like to quote the chief executive officer, the person who makes all the day-to-day decisions at the company. Sometimes a public relations person does the talking, but good reporters quote them as a last resort.

- *Board members:* While this doesn't happen often, members of a company's board of directors, who supervise the actions of the top officers of the company, will talk about corporate events.

- *Employees:* Sometimes workers talk about corporate events, particularly when jobs are added or lost.

- *Academics:* Top teachers in marketing, management, accounting, and other business disciplines observe companies' events and comment on them from a distance. They are not direct stakeholders in the business but can be credible sources because they're able to add context with their business expertise.

- *Market forecasters:* Economists and market analysts within brokerage firms who look at economic and business fundamentals to predict the future direction of the markets.

- *Analysts:* Research staffers at large brokerages who make recommendations to their traders and customers on whether to buy, sell, or hold a stock.

Watching the Stock-Watchers

Let's talk first about the last folks on the list, the analysts.

A stock analyst is a professional at an investment firm who analyzes the performance of specific companies. Analysts are considered experts in the industries they cover, and they write reports on the performance of companies within those sectors, based on their research.

However, it's important to know that these analysts work for brokerage houses that might have a stake in the company being researched, either because the brokerage holds shares in its own account or because brokerages have investment banking divisions that help take private companies public. While good analysts disclose these facts—and reporters should always ask about their firm's stock positions beforehand—it's always good to know this information at the outset.

From the way analysts are quoted in print and showcased on TV, you would think their role is to educate the public. That's not their job. Analysts do the dirty work of sifting through much of the research data covered in Chapter 4 to determine winning stocks in an industry. But their first duty is to their employers, brokerages that sell stock to investors and may also make a business in helping corporations go public or sell new issues of their publicly traded stock to investors. Analysts support the sales operation of a brokerage by developing research that helps institutional and individual stockbrokers who work at their firm to market stock to investors.

If you hear about a company going public, you should know that analysts are part of the service force that creates a "buzz" about that company's operations before it offers stock and well after the process.

"It's very important to understand how an underwriter [an investment banker with a brokerage unit] plans to service your issue during the entire IPO process and how that selling effort will continue after you go public," says Pete Scott, chief financial officer of Berringer Wine Estates, the Napa, California–based winemaker that went public last year. "That involves having an analyst force that keeps researching your stock and keeps your name out there for shareholders."

Yet before anyone jumps to the conclusion that analysts get away with "touting" stocks their employers have a stake in, the marketplace provides a natural check and balance. Remember that analysts need to provide accurate research so their employers can decide whether to sell the stock of the company the analyst is covering. Brokerages typically buy promising shares for their own accounts, and like you or me, they like to see those shares go up, not down. Inaccurate research eventually gets discovered, and no one wants to be in the position of losing money on a stock with inflated projections. Also, an investment firm's credibility on the street would be nil. Despite what you hear about cutthroat capitalism, lying generally isn't very good for business.

Often, analysts are the unpopular folks within brokerages who may detect the first signs of trouble in a business which will affect the stock price for all investors, including their employers. That is also their job.

RESEARCH TIP: ANALYZING THE ANALYSTS

It's possible to check out the credentials and track records of analysts who watch stocks that you're watching. First, to identify all the analysts who watch your stock, see if your library has the latest copy of the *Nelson Guide for Investment Research*. Each year, Nelson updates its list of analysts covering every public company. Also, bookmark Zack's Investment Research on your computer (the address is in Chapter 10) for the latest consensus on earnings forecasts for your company.

What the Market Forecaster Does

Ever hear the names Abby Joseph Cohen or Elaine Garzarelli? These two women represent the highest echelon of Wall Street pundits and have since October 19, 1987, the so-called Black Monday crash during which the DJIA fell 508 points, or 22.6 percent. Interestingly, Black Monday, which took the DJIA down to a now-distant 1738.74 level, turned out to be only a breather for the market's current march to 12,000.

Garzarelli, now head of her own Chicago-based investment firm, has continued to make public-relations hay out of her insightful prediction 12 years ago. But Cohen, whom we met in Chapter 5, is now credited with having the best crystal ball on Wall Street. She is managing director at Goldman, Sachs & Co.

Cohen credits her market forecasts to fundamental analysis, what value investors practice. "We look at what's going on in the economy, with companies, and what's going on globally," she told *Business Week* in a 1996 article. "We then look at how securities are valued and if they are attractive given the economic environment. Finally, we also look at fund flows in and out of markets." Cohen said she uses computer models only sparingly. "My first job was as a junior economist at the Fed, and I learned right away that models blow up if the economic environment changes."

Even though Warren Buffett says he makes his stock decisions largely independently of the course of markets and economic forecasts, Cohen's approach seems to be based on the basic fundamental analysis most value investors use. So it will be interesting to see where those methods take her.

Pundits Under Fire

With the rapid-fire pace of today's media coverage, the drive for fresh investment information, opinion, and news is the most competitive it's ever been. And with that second-by-second demand comes a heightened chance for error and misinterpretation.

A recent example on the cable television network CNBC shows the danger investment experts face with off-the-cuff remarks going out to investors hungry for information. On December 2, 1998, James J. Cramer, a money manager, columnist, and regular CNBC commentator, was discussing Wavephone, an Internet data broadcasting company. He referred to Wavephone, whose stock had risen 60 percent the previous trading session, as an example of what he termed "fraud-u-net companies," saying that he had talked with a broker that morning about the possibilities of short-selling Wavephone's stock, essentially placing a bet that the stock would fall.

Wavephone executives protested Cramer's comments after the value of their stock went from a December 1 close of $15.25 a share to a close of $8.0625 after Cramer's broadcast. Cramer was temporarily suspended from the CNBC program "Squawk Box" until he agreed to edit his comments.

CNBC's policy, as with many journalistic organizations, is to fully disclose its sources' connections. But while Cramer clearly stated he had no plans to short Wavephone stocks, he stated in a followup column, "Saying that a money manager must never discuss stocks because it is hopefully conflicted is a head-in-the-sand mentality that would deny investors substantive information from those actually in the business."

The bottom line: Freedom of information is a good thing. But there is plenty of information out there, and the only way to judge it is to not make a snap decision based on the first version of what you hear. And do what good reporters do: Try to get at least two sources to confirm a fact before you act.

Putting It All Together

When to Sell

How to Review Your Portfolio for Changes

And you thought it was tough figuring out how to *buy* a stock. Figuring out when to sell can be agonizing if you don't have a clear picture in your mind of the goals you sought to accomplish when you bought the stock. If you followed the basic Graham principles, you knew when you bought the company what its full per-share value would be, so you should be prepared for this moment.

But sometimes we get close to our stocks, like a good dog or your first really great car. If you found a bargain ten years ago that's done well for you and made you look like a genius at cocktail parties, it's tough to say goodbye when all your meters register "sell." But that's exactly the point: The accuracy of your forecasts got you here in the first place, so maybe it's time to take a profit and plow some money back into the next investment that makes you look smart.

The world changes, fortunately or unfortunately for you. Circumstances change for companies, even those whose management plans well for the future. It is why Warren Buffett, whose lifetime average annual investment gain stands between 20 and 30 percent, makes mistakes sometimes. Of course, sometimes circumstances change in favor of a company, and you may decide the original sale target you had in mind might go a lot higher.

We'll get to specific points about triggering a sale of your stock, but first, let's review a few points made in Chapter 5 when we talked about setting up your portfolio:

- *Value investors aren't traders.*   That's to say that you, the value investor, get into a stock for the long haul. You don't buy today and sell next week. That's not how you nurture your goals. Therefore, a conscientious value investor conducts regular reviews of the numbers and the news that affect his stocks and adjusts his battle plan accordingly. Come to think of it, that's what a good CEO does.

- *Never forget your personal investment goals.*   So one of your stocks heads down or up suddenly. Whether you are 30 years away from retirement, or 3 months, it always pays to take some time to reevaluate your ownership of this company, and remember, as a shareholder, you are a part owner in this company. But if you believe in your stake, based on the strength of your computations and qualitative judgments about the company, stick with it until you feel it's appropriate to sell—or buy more. And, of course, keep an eye on your tax situation to make sure your sale won't affect your finances adversely. It might feel great to take that profit, but not if a big chunk is going to Uncle Sam.

- *Don't believe the Dow.*   There's no question that broad market measuring sticks like the Dow Jones industrial average, the Standard & Poor's 500, and the NASDAQ indices are bellwethers and give us a worthwhile view of investor optimism and pessimism. But if you pick a good company with solid prospects and fundamentals, the swings in these markets really shouldn't influence your choice. If you're going to look for marketplace issues that really do affect your stock, look at the economy, particularly the path of interest rates. If it costs companies and consumers too much to borrow, they might not be able to buy as much from your company. Stick to signals that directly affect your company's operations, and minimize the rest.

  If we find a company we like, the level of the market will not really impact our decisions. We will decide company by company. We spend essentially no time thinking about macroeconomic factors. In other words, if somebody handed us a prediction by the most revered intellectual on the subject, with figures for unemployment or interest rates or whatever it might be for the next two years, we would not pay any attention to it. We simply try to focus on businesses that we think we understand and where we like the price and management.[1]

In his rare speeches and pronouncements, Warren Buffett— quoted above— will often trot out a fictional character called "Mr. Market." This individual is the personification of everything the Oracle of Omaha hates about the tendency of many investors to react to the market, not the businesses they have purchased. Mr. Market jumps when the Dow does; he also heads south when the Dow does.

It's tough not to sympathize with Mr. Market on days when the Dow slides 300 points or rises 250, but there are more important signals for value investors to consider selling.

Graham's Approach

If a stock rises 50 percent in value (in this case meaning the market price), it might be a good time to consider selling. Or if you've set another target above or below this 50-percent rule and your projections indicate it won't go higher and may drop, it's time to get out.

It's an interesting position that Graham took here, because many technical analysts (the scourge of value investors for their reliance on market timing techniques) take the same position. But before you do anything, go back to your tools of fundamental analysis, assess your current financial goals, and see where you really stand. If, based on your calculations, this company has achieved its full value for a while and you have a sensible place for this profit to go, sell. If you think the stock still has unrecognized value, hang on.

How Much Profit to Take

If you're borderline on a sale even after you go back to the fundamentals, the American Association of Individual Investors has a great suggestion.

Figure out how much money it would take to cover your initial investment in the stock (that's stock price, commission, and capital gains tax from a sale) and cash in that amount of stock. You've covered your initial nut, so you haven't lost anything. Then you can watch the remainder of the shares in that investment to see if their value will continue to climb.

Selling on Bad News

As a value investor, you're looking for news that will affect the assets and income of your company, so you want to be attuned to earnings projections and competitive issues that affect your stock. As information about investing has exploded on almost every medium that exists, news about companies has become tremendously competitive. The nature of business journalism is to "break" news before the company does, to be first with the story. But here's a warning: If you hear that your company's earnings are going to be down or up, *always consider the source.* Is the company stating it will have lower earnings, or is it a rumor or just an aggressive analyst downgrading his earnings projections on your company? Not that analysts don't know their stuff, but it always helps to know the analyst's record.

Sometimes if you see your stock getting clobbered, it's tough to fight the temptation to run to the phone or keyboard to tell your broker to sell before you lose a considerable portion of your investment. But you need to learn to watch the people whose words may have a direct impact on your investment. Occasionally, bad news can be a great chance to buy more shares of a company with solid fundamentals.

Working with Stop-Loss Orders

Example: Let's say you bought a stock at $15 and it is now trading at $30, but you're not sure if it will go higher. You decide to place an order to sell (a stop-loss) at $24 (which would represent a 20-percent drop). This way, you preserve 80 percent of your initial gain, less commission.

Value investors never buy stock with the expectation that the shares are going to plummet. That's a job for so-called short-sellers, who profit by borrowing money to buy stocks they expect to drop in price. But if you have concern that news might send your stock through the floor (something value investors should have a handle on through regular reviews of their analysis), it never hurts to tell your broker that you want to sell if your stock drops to a certain price. Of course, the downside is that the company can plummet one day, and you sell automatically, and then recover to previous or higher levels the next. So keep on top of the news and make sure any automatic order to sell or buy is updated based on your analysis.

Selling for Size

Assume a stock you bought years ago now makes up anywhere from 10 to 50 percent of your portfolio. Some investors believe that you shouldn't have more than 20 percent of your total portfolio value in any single investment. That in itself is a good trigger point for closer analysis of whether the stock should be kept. But should you sell regardless? Consider:

- Do your numbers show whether this stock will rise safely, making your overall portfolio more valuable over time? If you are confident that this stock, through reinvested dividends, splits, and your additional purchases, will be worth a nice chunk for you and your heirs someday, you may not want to sell right now.

- If you sell a portion of this investment now, do you have another investment in mind that is trading below its value? If so, it might be worth cashing out a little and diversifying more.

- How soon will you need this money? A general rule of thumb is that if you believe you will need the value of your investment within three years, you might be wiser to move it into more conservative fixed-rate investments or cash.

Logging On

Trusting What's Online and on the Software Shelves

There's no better time to be a beginning investor than today, particularly if you own a computer with a modem. Most major business magazines and newspapers have online sites with archives you can check for news on a company. Investment firms have archival sites that you can tap for investment research over the years. And there are now dozens of websites that help you screen and chart investments.

On the software side, there are dozens of consumer investment programs. But aside from those that help you manage your finances and keep track of your investments, such as Quicken or Microsoft Money, this book does not endorse any specific stock-screening program. The reason? Most PC software programs can help you screen stocks with formulas built into their databases, but you still have to do your homework finding data and researching corporate history to cover the other basics of fundamental research. We'll take a look at the right things to look for in a program instead.

Respected services like Value Line now have software and online products you can use to help you examine investments, but they're not cheap.

If you're starting out, it's best to see what types of information you can collect for free. After all, why let the process of learning about investing detract from your profits? For Value Line, a valuable research source for anyone investing their money, it's worth a trip to the public library to photocopy hard copies of the research. That's because the published product and the electronic resources they have aren't cheap, and it makes sense to get the hang of using them before you spend the money.[1] In addition, many online services and websites offer basic stock-screening programs that let you narrow down your choices of stock for free.

What Investment Software Can Do for Investors...And What It Can't

Before angry software manufacturers start protesting, let's go to the experts for some commentary on what consumer computer software can do.

1. *Consumer stock programs are far less sophisticated than what the professionals use.* All of the investment professionals interviewed in Chapter 2 use computer software programs that cost hundreds, sometimes thousands of dollars after they are configured to meet those professionals' respective screening and mathematical criteria. Software programs off the shelf don't give you that many options, and in all honesty, you may not have the time to use them anyway. The American Association of Individual Investors points out that most (but not all) of the commercially available fundamental investment programs are designed to screen data rather than judge a security's worth on the basis of fundamental valuation principles. There are now a number of programs on the market that will screen a data set of 1000 to 10,000 companies on any number of fundamental variables. Typically, these programs come with their own data, and the scope of the coverage is determined by the database the software uses.

2. *Stock screening software is useful, but it has its limits.* The AAII gives an example of how screening software works. Pick an indicator, such as a low price-to-book ratio. The investor could decide to screen a database for companies with a market value of between $20 million and $100 million. In addition, the investor might look for those stocks in this group whose price-to-book ratios are low, say, below 1.0. The screening program could go through the database rapidly and select the companies that meet these criteria. Of course, once the stocks are selected, the investor must always look further at the individual companies before

making any investment. There are many important judgment factors that the computer cannot analyze. You do that.

A problem with this is that you get a pileup of stocks without any real *ranking* of criteria.

In any event, a good screening program should give you access to a large database and the flexibility to create different criteria for screening. You should not be locked into preset criteria. The program should allow transfer of data to other applications, such as a spreadsheet program. Without this latter capability, you cannot perform further analysis essential for effective security selection.

3. *Portfolio management software has its limitations too.*   There are freestanding programs to maintain your account records and analyze characteristics of a portfolio, but programs like Quicken and Money have portfolio capability that will do the basics of record keeping. The problem with many portfolio management software programs is they don't always have the best tools to measure overall performance. So again, you may want to set a time of the year or quarter to rerun your formulas.

Software-Buying Checklist (AAII)

- Make sure the database (online or on disk; online access is preferable because it's more current) has a wide universe of stocks to choose from.
- Make sure there's real depth of information as far as different ratio and formula measurements to screen from and access to recent investment research.
- Make sure you know where to get instant updates of all that material (again, make sure there's an online component to update this program).
- Make sure you're buying software compatible with your computer (in recent years, many investment programs have abandoned Apple Computer's operating system platform in favor of the PC-based Windows environment).
- Decide whether you're going to be able to recover the price of your software in investment gains. It doesn't make any sense to load up on equipment to pick winners if the cost of the equipment is going to eat up your profits. If that's the case, take paper, pencil, and a calculator to the public library and do your work there.

The process of portfolio management is more than mere record-keeping. It should analyze total portfolio wealth allocation. Investors should also be interested in determining insurance needs, cash and security holdings that are appropriate for their lifestyles, financial needs, income, and overall wealth. Internal rate of return (IRR) is the appropriate value-weighted measure of portfolio return. This is the rate of return needed each period, to make the ending value of your portfolio at least match the starting value, with full accounting for cash withdrawals and deposits. This measure can be compared to market returns to determine whether you are earning a sufficient return. See if the program you are considering buying focuses on this issue.

Also, portfolio management software should be able to deal with the reinvestment of dividends or other income and be able to account for the changes in returns. It should also have the capability of handling not only all your current investments but also any investment vehicle you might consider in the future.

Good portfolio management software should make taxes easier as well, helping you keep a record of basis prices even when you've added and subtracted many times from a portfolio over the years. Most portfolio management programs will prepare tax schedules B and D, which list interest and dividend income and capital gains and losses. If the program does not actually prepare a tax return, it should be able to group information for you to use on a printed return or with another program. Again, Internet capability is very helpful here because the ability to link to an online database to obtain current price information for portfolio updating is crucial at tax time.

Quicken '99 vs. Microsoft Money '99: CNet's Shootout

CNet, a leading online resource/review center for all things related to computers, did this 1998 comparison of the 1999 editions of the two leading personal finance programs, Intuit's Quicken and Microsoft Money. Here are some highlights of what they found.[2]

Checking: When it comes to the checkbook, Quicken is tough to beat. Whether you write a simple check via the onscreen checkbook (which still resembles the real thing), split a transaction between sev-

Quicken '99 vs. Microsoft Money '99: CNet's Shootout *(Continued)*

eral categories, balance an account, or generate a report, Quicken handles the chore quickly, and the software never gets in the way. As a testament to the thoroughness of this electronic checkbook, little has changed from last year. So what has? Now you can sort a reconciliation display by two more criteria (payee and amount), and Quicken's reports are organized a bit better. Tax-oriented reports, for example, are now grouped together rather than spread under two different headings.

Portfolio organization: Quicken's investment acumen still outshines Money's. Its portfolio presentation hasn't changed, and investments still appear in a nifty table-style format, which you can track with an amazing assortment of criteria and even organize into custom views. Also, Quicken includes all the transaction types necessary for you to track a complex portfolio, including corporate acquisitions and stock splits. One of the few modifications is that Quicken, like Money, now lets you use Web-based stock and fund search tools rather than storing them on your machine. Also new is that you can download up to five years of quotes to flesh out your records, as Quicken to assign asset allocation categories to securities, or sync the Quicken portfolio on your hard drive with the one at Quicken.com. And don't forget its handy capital gains estimator, which "what-ifs" possible security sales.

Expense tracking: We still can't fathom Money's fixation for paying bills with all-purpose forms instead of something that really looks like a check. But if you can get past that quirk, this program's checkbook and bill-paying skills now match Quicken's. Give most of the credit to Money's Bill & Deposit section, which makes it much easier to schedule recurring bills. And Money's register itself now includes both current and ending balances and lets you sort the reconciliation display to better match the paper statement from your bank. Plus, Money's built-in reports—about the same number as Quicken—still include the excellent monthly overview, which Quicken would be smart to duplicate.

Investment tracking: When it comes to investment, Money '99, like Quicken, more or less rests on its laurels. It sports the same portfolio

---

Quicken '99 vs. Microsoft Money '99: CNet's Shootout (*Continued*)

views here as it did last year: performance, holdings, quotes, fundamentals, positions, and allocation. But the investment area now lets you create a "watch list" of stocks or funds that you want to track, even if you don't own a share. It's also easy to track employee stock options with Money. (It's probably not a coincidence that Microsoft, a company whose employees become millionaires on options, is the first to debut such a feature.) Money displays stocks intelligently, shows you details when you ask for them, and links the portfolio data on your hard drive with the portfolio you keep at Microsoft's online financial site, Microsoft Investor, just as smoothly as Quicken does. In fact, Money's investment tools integrate your PC and the Web more powerfully than Quicken's, though last year's problem remains: after a six-month free trial, you must pay $9.95 per month to access all of Investor (Microsoft's financial site).

Retirement planning: This year, Quicken doesn't leave you up the proverbial creek without a planning paddle. Its new QuickPlan (a truncated version of the Quicken Financial Planner program) takes you through basic retirement planning, asking questions about your current portfolio and your retirement expectations. But QuickPlan fails to factor in major life events, such as career changes or college savings, and ultimately, it's feeble compared to Money's primo planner. Also new is that Quicken's three intriguing What If? scenarios blend disk and Web resources to help you explore college tuition costs, estate planning, and home buying. You'll be able to download more scenarios from Quicken.com in the future, Intuit says. Quicken retains its Debt Reduction Planner, which can finally ignore mortgage loans (if you ask it to) and concentrate on short-term debt, such as credit cards.

Taxes: Speaking of debt, when tax time comes, Quicken '99 is your best friend. That's because it entitles you to one free return prepared by WebTurboTax, Intuit's Web-based tax prep service (last year, the cost was $9.95 per return). If your taxes are too complex for TurboTax (Intuit says it will handle more involved returns this year), you can fall back on Quicken's standbys, TaxPlanner, which grabs numbers from your records and calculates current liability, and Deduction Finder. Welcome tax-related additions this year include a

---

Quicken '99 vs. Microsoft Money '99: CNet's Shootout (*Continued*)

capital gains What If? tool that shows the tax ramifications of selling securities, and Quicken's newfound ability to guess your tax classification based on your entry in the check's category field.

If there's one area where Money '99 falls far short, though, it's taxes. What little tax help this program does provide seems more like an afterthought than something fully thought out. Its new tax deduction finder, though welcome, pales in comparison to Quicken's, especially in ease of use. On the upside, its Tax Estimator is still solid—better than Quicken's planner in fact. It's always up-to-date, since it automatically grabs data from Money's records. But its lack of sophisticated tax advice or, better yet, tax preparation à la Turbo-Tax Online is even more glaring this year.

General financial planning: No surprises here. Like its forebear, Money '99 holds Quicken in a planning headlock. Where Quicken Deluxe boasts only a basic financial planner, Money builds on last year's impressive debut. Its renamed Lifetime Planner simply kicks butt. By the time you wend your way through its questionnairelike process, you'll know not only whether you'll have enough money for your golden years but also when you should expect tough times ahead (for example, when all the kids are attending college at once). To top it off, Money has revised its Budget Planner (it's a lot simpler to use, better than Quicken's, and motivates you to actually plan a budget for once) and retains its thorough Debt Reduction Planner.

What the Internet Can Do for Investors...And What It Can't

By the year 2000, many Internet experts think 60 million people, more than a quarter of the nation's population, will be online. And they note that's a *conservative* estimate.

Of course, if you're computerphobic or don't have the money right now to buy a home computer, it certainly doesn't mean you're out of luck in today's investing world. As we've stated often in this book, most of the resources that can help you most, from annual reports to Value Line research, are free of charge at your local public library.

But surfing the Internet for investment information is a good way to find basic information fast, if you know the best and most accurate ways and places to look.

Accuracy on the Net Is a Big Issue

You read all the time about Internet chatrooms where people tell their deepest, darkest secrets online but have absolutely no idea who they're really dealing with. Well, that's the way you have to view any investment information you receive online. Always double-click with a healthy dose of suspicion and the requirement to always verify the sources of your information.

Any good investor not hooked up to a computer would do the same thing, of course. If goes back to that old, useful adage: Don't believe everything you read.

But the Internet provides a particular problem average investors have never seen before; the blinding speed of the technology means the people and companies who put the information on the Internet have to do it *fast*. And the trouble with speed is that sometimes things get sloppy.

An informal study of a half dozen stocks conducted by NASD Regulation, Inc. (NASDR) showed a close correlation between Internet postings and changes in both trading volume and price, which causes problems for regulators.[3] While NASDR—which represents the National Association of Securities Dealers, or NASDAQ, members—will aggressively pursue securities fraud or stock manipulation perpetrated on the Internet, it's nearly impossible to monitor investment-related postings at thousands of chatrooms, bulletin boards, newsgroups, and homepages. And since NASD and other exchanges can only police members who do wrong, the opportunities for online investment scam artists have increased exponentially.

The investor's top government watchdog, the Securities and Exchange Commission, has similar problems. The government's people and technology resources can only go so far, and the growth of the Internet into a popular communications medium hasn't been happening for that many years. Regulators can't keep up with the way the Internet changes every day, and as more people sign on, that's going to make the task even more difficult.

In simplest terms, good luck finding an actual paper trail that will help you prosecute online criminals.

An Online Accuracy Checklist

- *Screen online brokers.*   When considering using an online broker, take a close look at the site and its fine print. Then don't be afraid to pick up the phone and call them with questions. Also, you can do a search of various regulatory agencies and business publications to find out if a particular online broker has been challenged in court or by the government for any reason. Also, since most brokerages settle customer disputes by arbitration these days, ask the online brokerage to explain how these arbitrations are handled. If you can't find someone to explain this to you, hang up and go to a brokerage that has a good answer ready for you, even if it means going to a traditional, full-service brokerage.

- *Question all bulletin board and chatroom services.*   Again, you don't know who's really behind the message. Is the person giving you advice or news on a particular investment a licensed broker or a scam artist? It's virtually impossible to find out. Chatrooms are fun, but you're going to find the real information you need from established investment sources.

- *Know a scammer's language.*   Would you invest in a "can't-miss opportunity" plastered on a highway billboard? Some of these computerized investment pitches have just about as much credibility. Rumors are rampant in the financial market and always have been. But if someone touts "inside information" on a "once-in-a-lifetime opportunity" based on a merger or acquisition "that's just about to break," take a step back and ask yourself who's giving you this information. Reputable sources of information don't talk this way, and generally, their speculation is labeled as just that. Never accept rumor as fact, particularly when it's your money.

If You Get Suspicious, Here's Who to Call

As stated above, these regulatory agencies have their hands full with plenty of scam artists who haven't even tried the Internet yet. But if you report something questionable, chances are these agencies can publicize the scenario so other investors don't get hurt.

NASD Regulation, Inc.
1735 K Street, NW
Washington, DC 20006-1506
(301) 590-6500; (800) 289-9999
(http://www.nasdr.com)

U.S. Securities and Exchange Commission
Office of Investor Education and Assistance
450 5th Street, NW
Washington, DC 20549
(202) 942-4108; TTD (202) 942-7065
(http://www.sec.gov)

For the telephone number of your state securities regulator:
North American Securities Administrators Association, Inc.
One Massachusetts Avenue, NW
Suite 310
Washington, DC 20001
(202) 737-0900

Surfing for Value
A List of Useful Websites for Value Investors

M ost of the following websites deal with stock investing, but in the interest of managing *all* of your money, there are also useful sites for mutual funds, borrowing, bank savings rates, and consumer product testing.

Online brokerages can be accessed through most of these sites too (Figure 10-1), but you want to compare offerings before you sign on at any online brokerage.

It's important to note that website addresses (the www listings) change from time to time, and if you can't find a website listed with any of the addresses below, then refer to a search engine like Yahoo!, HotBot, or Lycos to see if the site has moved to a new address. If you can't find it through the search engines, it is possible the site has been discontinued since publication of this book.

Amazon.com (http://www.amazon.com) Wherever you end up buying the book, Amazon.com is a good place to start a topic search for any financial subject you're interested in learning about.

Online Trades: Who Handles the Most?	
Charles Schwab	29%
E*Trade	11%
Fidelity	9%
Waterhouse	9%
Datek	8%
Ameritrade	7%
Others	27%

FIGURE 10-1 Online Trades. (*Source:* Internet World, Piper Jaffray, 1998.)

America Online (http://www.aol.com) This online service is a good place for beginners to learn about the web and investing. AOL's personal finance page has great resources for researching stocks, charting, keeping track of purchases, and screening investments as you get more comfortable with your own parameters for purchase. For pricing information based on the number of hours you expect to be online, call (800) 540-9449.

American Association for Individual Investors (http://www.aaii. com) This Chicago-based organization serves the needs of beginning and experienced individual investors. Has great tutorials.

Bank Rate Monitor (http://www.bankrate.com) One of the best and most reliable places to get rates on auto loans, credit cards, mortgages, CDs, and more.

BARRA Portfolio (http://www.barra.com) A great place to look for charts on all the major indexes, plus their plotting points in case you want to design charts yourself.

BigCharts (http://www.bigcharts.com) One of the coolest sites on the Web for charting individual investment performance. This free site, sponsored by major brokerages, allows you to compare a chosen stock's performance against other stocks in its class, other major indexes, and on the basis of key ratios like P/E. Definitely worth bookmarking.

Bloomberg Online (http://www.bloomberg.com) Not as handy as the private terminals Bloomberg sells to brokerages, but market news is always up-to-date, and key charting information can be found here.

FIGURE 10-2 BigCharts Logo. (*Source:* BigCharts Service)

FIGURE 10-3 Bloomberg Logo.

Business Week **Online** (http://www.businessweek.com) One of the leading business publications in the country. It has a wonderful free archive for researching stocks based on news from the last few years. All you have to do is register.

Compare.Net (http://www.comparenet.com) If you're considering using an online broker, take a look at this site to sift through features and prices. It's a consumer site that focuses on pricing and features for services, automobiles, electronics, and other things we buy. Worth a look.

Disclosure (http://www.disclosure.com) The easiest way to get to SEC documents on particular companies; it even beats the SEC's own online database, EDGAR.

Fidelity Investments (http://personal71.fidelity.com/misc/demos) Obviously, Fidelity wants to sell you mutual funds, but they've got one of the best design-your-own-portfolio sites. They take you through a questionnaire that measures your assets and risk tolerance, and with a click of a button, it gives you an asset allocation portfolio with the types of investments that best suit your current situation. It's fun, it doesn't take much time, and you log off with some good ideas.

Global Financial Data (http://www.globalfindata.com) Interested in finding stock market data from the early part of the century up to now? This is a great site for historical market data of all stripes.

FIGURE 10-4 Hoover's Logo.

Hoover's Business Resources (http://www.hoovers.com) A great online source for independent company research. Detailed profiles on 2500 companies; basic stats on 10,000 more. It charges subscription fees for more detailed reports, though.

Investment Company Institute (http://www.ici.org/new.html) Ever wonder where all that money pouring into mutual funds is going? This industry association provides regular weekly tracking data for the types of mutual funds that are gaining—and losing—investment dollars. Gives you insight on what categories of funds are most popular.

Investor's Business Daily (http://www.investors.com) The national daily business newspaper for top-level executives and investors. (Keyword: IBD). Great charts.

Looksmart (http://www.looksmart.com) Not that value investors base their selections that heavily on past markets or the economy, but this is a great site for finding out official data on spending, the economy, investing, interest rates, census reports, and marketing demographics.

Media Logic (http://www.mlinet.com) This great site is a warehouse of information on virtually every aspect of investing, markets, or economic trends. Dozens upon dozens of links to trading records for equities, currencies, metals, notes, and bonds. A great place to get lost.

Market Guide's Stock Reports (http://research.web.aol.com/marketguide.html) This is a site on America Online, but you don't have to be a subscriber to get there. It contains fundamental financial information on over 10,000 U.S. and foreign companies, and you can reach Morningstar from there too.

Moneysearch.com (http://www.moneysearch.com) A good site that helps you search for information on practically any area of investing. Also has links to various publications and sites that might prove useful for a beginning investor.

FIGURE 10-5 Moneysearch Logo.

The Motley Fool (http://www.fool.com) A good site for tutorials and up-to-date research and commentary on investments. The chat isn't bad either.

NASDAQ (http://www.nasdaq.com/reference/onlinemarkets.stm) this particular page gives you links to virtually any exchange in the world—stock, commodity, or futures. It might be worth telling your kids about in case they have to study the markets in school.

National Association of Investors Corp. (http://www.better-investing. org) Ever wonder where the Beardstown Ladies went to get their investment club started? These are the folks. This nationwide organization provides regular advisory services to investment clubs, and their stock valuation system is second to none for beginning investors. A worthwhile contact for individuals or groups. NAIC members get lots of practice working formulas and doing their own fundamental research.

New York Stock Exchange (http://www.nyse.com) Up-to-the-moment quotes from the floor of the NYSE. Also some good investment basics listed on this site.

Ohio State Financial Website (http://www.cob.ohio-state.edu/~fin/osudata.htm) This is a great find. It's a hodgepodge of investment, economic, and corporate sites with great locations for charts, graphs, back information on companies, and projection data. Give yourself an hour or so to surf it, and get ready to bookmark!

OnlineInvestor.com (http://www.onlineinvestor.com) Great clearinghouse for online brokers and good screening programs for stocks. Also contains good links to all forms of financial information.

PRNewswire (http://www.prnewswire.com) Don't let the name throw you. This site is a great place to find company press releases on

FIGURE 10-6 Ohio State Logo.

earnings and other news that investors want to know about. It also has links to sites where you can order annual reports and other investor information.

Quicken.com (http://www.quicken.com) You don't have to own the wildly popular personal finance software to get something out of this site. It has a really great stock search page to give you some ideas for investments to study and has great commentary on other personal finance issues, such as insurance, college, and retirement planning. Definitely worth bookmarking.

Realtor.com (http://www.realtor.com) A great place to start your search for a home in any market in the country. Also a great mortgage rate database.

Standard & Poor's (http://www.stockinfo.standardpoor.com) A free site that gives you access to the longtime market analysis giant's stock reports and earnings news. Worth bookmarking if you don't have time to check the published S&P reports at the library.

Value Line (http://www.valueline.com) These guys are smart; they don't give anything away for free. This is an informational site that will tell you about the Value Line company and what it offers. Too bad—you can't download stock information here. You have to buy the hard copies that come in the mail or go to the library and photocopy the pages you need to work with.

Warren Buffett & Investing (http://www.global-omebiz.com/warrenbuffett.html) It's only appropriate that one of the greatest investors in history has a tribute site. Mr. Buffett has nothing to do with this location, but it contains some interesting links and archived stories to help you learn more about this guy.

The Web Investor (http://www.thewebinvestor.com) A good site for basic market news and earnings information you can use in examining stocks. Good international sites as well.

TheStreet.com (http://www.thestreet.com) The funny TV ads are correct. This site is a place for market and personal finance junkies. AOL

FIGURE 10-7 TheStreet.com Logo.

subscribers get a watered-down site for free, but to get the whole Magilla, it's $10 a month. Generally, it gives you the full range of ratio, market price, and research information you get at any good market information site, plus the articles on markets, investing, and tax issues are thought-provoking and written with flair. Everyone working for this site drinks a little too much coffee, which means the prose can be a little in-your-face, but that's not all bad either.

Zack's Earnings & Estimates (http://www.zacks.com) One of the best resources for earnings research that directly influences future stock prices. It surveys analysts—those who watch particular stocks on a full-time basis—to get their viewpoints on upcoming earnings and then publishes a market consensus for virtually every stock traded. Don't fail to check these numbers before you invest.

CHAPTER 11

Big-Picture Portfolios

How Age, Lifestyle, and Risk Tolerance Determine How to Allocate Investment Assets

This book has been about developing a value approach to investing and the theories and mindset you use to get there. But it would be wrong to leave the discussion without a few real-life examples of how asset allocation enters into the picture.

What Is Asset Allocation?

Asset allocation is what makes an overall investment strategy work. It involves the mixture of different categories of investments in a single portfolio to ensure adequate growth and offset risk, based on the investor's age and circumstances. Graham, who wrote his first two best-sellers in the 1930s and 1940s, advised particular mixtures of stocks and bonds based on the age of the investor.

In the 1990s, we have the world of mutual funds, grouped pools of securities and cash investments, each with its own asset allocation strategy revolving around the expertise of a portfolio manager. There is a dizzying number of choices for investors to choose from in both fund and individual investments. But value principles should still determine an investor's choices.

Why Different Types of Investments Are Necessary

It's one thing to talk about managing risk; it's another to see it in action.

The last major bear market in the early 1970s and the market crash of 1987 showed that investors who practiced asset allocation lost money, but not as badly as those who invested solely in stocks.

Diversification is good common sense, but there's an emotional component of investing that shouldn't be ignored, the individual's tolerance for risk.

Very few people think about risk when the market is flying high. Let the market drop a few hundred points, however, and risk and loss are on everyone's radar screen.

As we've mentioned several times in this book, there is no single *right* way to assemble a portfolio. But the following scenarios, based on opinions from several investment management firms, might give you some guidance.

Scenario 1: Dennis

Dennis, 29, is single and still in the early stages of his marketing career. He wants to begin putting something away for the future but finds that saving isn't so easy. Nevertheless, he has some money in a bank savings account and has begun contributing a small percentage of his pay to his employer's 401(k) plan.

Dennis has decided—at least for now—that he won't be retiring for at least 30 years, so he can afford to commit a substantial portion of his savings to stocks for long-term growth. In fact, as an investor in the "accumulation" phase, i.e., with a long-term horizon, Dennis could place more of his savings in stocks. But he realizes he needs a balanced portfolio, so he keeps some of his assets in more conservative investments.

Dennis's target asset allocation mix: 80% stocks/20% bonds. *Young investors can take more risk since they have more time to accumulate earnings and won't need it for awhile.*

Scenario 2: Ann

Ann, 39, is newly divorced. She has no children and works as a computer consultant. Fortunately, she was able to use her split of the assets in her divorce to reinvest in a new condo, but she is concerned about having only $15,000 in savings and no formal investment plan set up for her retirement. She realizes she has some catching up to do. She wants to be able to work part-time during her retirement, but what concerns her is making sure she has enough money should she become sick in her old age.

Since she is not yet 40, isn't planning on retiring fully, and is willing to tolerate some risk, Ann's portfolio should take on a similar appearance to Dennis's.

Ann's target asset allocation mix: 75% stocks/25% bonds. *Investors who are older and need to accumulate assets quickly should still focus on stocks, but they should be thinking about safeguarding their principal. Also, women live longer, so they should focus on a longer lifespan, possibly well into their eighties if their health is good.*

Scenario 3: Jim and Kim

Jim and his wife, Kim, are both in their early fifties. Their mortgage is paid off, their daughter has graduated from college and moved away from home, and they have begun thinking about retiring. The couple—a writer and a marketing executive—has always invested the majority of Kim's savings in stocks for maximum growth potential. Now that Jim wants to retire to focus on screenwriting full-time, they want to make sure all of their assets aren't eaten up in the stock market should it fall.

Jim and Kim have discussed the time when they will begin drawing on their savings. During this "transition" phase—the years between accumulation and retirement—they have planned to gradually shift a portion of their savings into bonds and cash reserves. While risk has become a major consideration, they understand that investing for the future does not end at Jim's retirement. Therefore, as a means of maximizing their return, the couple plans to keep more than half of their savings in stocks, at least until Jim actually retires.

Jim and Kim's asset allocation mix: 60% stocks/40% bonds. *Middle-aged investors, depending on their post-retirement plans, need to slow* *down the growth cycle a little bit, shifting more of their assets into fixed-income investments that won't lose principal.*

Scenario 4: Phil and Robin

Since Phil and Robin have passed on their successful family photography business to their son M. J., most of their time has been spent relaxing at home and visiting with their friends, children, and grandchildren. Both in their early sixties, they want as comfortable a lifestyle as they enjoyed when they both were working. They've built a getaway cabin in Wisconsin, and they like to travel. Robin, however, has a nagging concern: She recalls that her parents, who lived well into their eighties, had to cut back on their living expenses after their retirement savings grew smaller and smaller with each passing year.

Now that they have retired, Robin and Phil need a stream of income to supplement their Social Security and pension benefits. Therefore, nearly half of their savings is invested in income-oriented bonds. To fight inflation, they've also kept a good portion of their assets in stocks. Based on current life expectancy, either Robin or Phil—or both—could live another 20 or 30 years. With that long an investment horizon, they are willing to accept the short-term risks associated with stocks in anticipation of their great long-term rewards.

Robin and Phil's asset allocation: 40% stocks/60% bonds. *As investors move into their senior years, they shouldn't forget that lifespan keeps growing, and with it the need for some growth in their portfolio.*

Scenario 5: Tom

Tom, a 78-year-old widower, has remained active since his retirement as a successful engineer some 15 years ago. During that time, he has watched inflation and rising medical costs eat away at the fixed incomes of his friends. Therefore, Tom wants to make certain that his savings support all of his future living and medical expenses.

Over the past several years, Tom has been slowly moving more of his savings into bonds for a higher income. However, because he has seen how inflation can reduce purchasing power over the long term, he keeps a small portion of his portfolio—some 20%—in stocks to protect his savings.

Some Very General Rules of Thumb: Portfolio Allocation

	Stocks (%)	Bonds (%)	Cash (%)
High-risk investors; young investors	70–80	15–25	0–5
Medium risk investors; investors approaching retirement	60	30–40	0–10
Low-risk investors; retiring investors and retirees	40–50	40–50	5–20
Investors over age 70	20–30	60	10–20

How These Portfolios Fare (Stocks%/Bonds%/Cash%)

	80/20/0	60/40/0	40/40/20	20/60/20
Average return (%)	9.5	8.5	7.3	6.0
Average loss (%)	−10.0	−8.0	−5.0	−3.0
Worst annual loss (%)	−36.0	−28.0	−19.0	−12.0
Bear market loss, 1973–74 (%)	−32.0	−22.0	−12.0	−3.0

Source: The Vanguard Retirement Guide, Irwin, 1996.

Tom's allocation: 20% stocks/80% bonds. *Just because you're moving into your seventies and eighties, don't put all your money into fixed-income investments if your health is good. You still need some protection from inflation for the years ahead.*

A comfortable retirement isn't the only reason to create an investment portfolio. College expenses for children are expected to reach more than $120,000 for the average four-year private university by 2010. And 24-hour nursing home care, currently averaging $40,000 per year, may rise as high as $70,000 a year in the next five years.

So investment planning involves much more than planning for retirement.

In summary, no one can select his or her investments solely from a computer program or the discovery of an asset found to be undervalued. Developing a long-term investing strategy means knowing yourself and the risks you want to take, while being able to make adjustments along the way.

chapter 12

Home Stretch

Going Over the Basics One More Time and the Forecast for Finding Value Ahead

I n mid-September 1998, Warren Buffett startled Wall Street with the disclosure that he had scraped together $9 billion in petty cash should market values ever come down to his liking.

Obviously, the Oracle was seeing a little trouble in his crystal ball. Sure enough, late that month, longtime Buffett darlings Coca-Cola, Gillette, and Procter & Gamble saw their stocks slide, as earnings were coming in under expectations. All three stocks saw double-digit drops in their stock prices going into the fall.

But though Buffett's move to cash shook up the market for a few days, Warren-watchers reminded themselves that the grizzled value investor comes off the sidelines when the news is bad. Because when news is bad, investments get cheap.

As he told a reporter during the bear market of 1974, "I feel like an oversexed guy in a harem. This is the time to start investing."[1]

Most of us would feel similarly amorous about market downturns if we had $9 billion in cash lying around. But there is a lesson here. If stormy weather is approaching, it's a good idea to start window-shopping and laying away a little money for when you find the right stocks at the right price. Then you can jump before the rest of the world figures it out.

One More Time: The Basics of Finding Value

- Remember that you're not buying a stock; you're buying a company. Act like an owner and you'll be a better investor.

- Be willing to study. Learn to pick apart corporate financial reports and use fundamental value calculations to tell you whether companies are undervalued or overvalued.

- Read the news. If you see news that affects your chosen company or the industry it's part of, pay close attention to see whether that news might affect future results.

- Always ask the question you would ask if you were buying an education, a home, or making any major investment: What is this worth now, and will its value increase in the future?

- Remember, there's strength in diversity. Learning to understand value investing from the perspective of stocks doesn't mean you can't apply the same principles to bonds, money market funds, or other investments. And remember to reassign your percentages in various assets based on your age and needs. That's asset allocation.

- Don't let the overall market throw you. The Dow Jones industrial average may be up 100 points one day, down 300 the next. How's your company doing? Do you know? If not, it's time to sit down with the numbers again.

- Assign yourself a specific week each year to review your investments. Sit down with your figures and assumptions and see if they still work. If not, make the necessary changes based on the same value principles.

Internet Stocks: Who Needs Fundamentals?

It's estimated that only 5 percent of Internet sites actually turn a profit, and those are dedicated to finance—or pornography. Yet if you looked at stock market returns any time during 1998 and into early 1999, you saw Internet stocks trading at stratospheric multiples with no end in sight.

In our initial discussion in Chapter 1 about money-losing Amazon.com—which analysts predicted could go as high as $400 a share or as low as $50—one wonders what Benjamin Graham would say if he were on the scene. Based on the items above, he would probably stay clear. But it would be great to hear his take on the intrinsic value of an Amazon.com or a Yahoo!

In fact, by late January 1999, investors were starting to look skeptically at the high values of Internet stocks. One investor's downturn might be another's buying opportunity, but on January 22, some Internet stocks were trading down as much as 50 percent of their value on New Year's Day.

Perhaps investors are starting to realize that earnings *are* important.

The Uncertainty Ahead

You were expecting some commentary on the *certainty* ahead? When it comes to the stock market, nothing is certain, especially at a time when so many individuals have so much to lose in a misstep. For the next year, the world economy will probably still be trying to shake off the "Asian contagion," the Clinton White House will still be trying to get over its Monica hangover, and Alan Greenspan will still be twisting his words into tight corkscrews and taking the market with him with every phrase.

That's why the value investor keeps his universe as small as possible, not ignorant of the world's events, but prepared enough so he or she can be independent of markets and the economy at large.

Happy hunting.

APPENDIX

A

Stock and Market Terms

Acid-Test Ratio: See *Quick Ratio.*

Accumulation Area: A term used in charting stocks, it indicates a time period during which a stock's price has remained in a relatively narrow range.

American Depositary Receipt (ADR): Used for foreign stocks, this receipt representing a share of stock in a foreign company is kept on deposit in a bank. The U.S. investor doesn't directly own the stock but owns the receipt representing the stock.

Annual Report: The report a publicly held company produces each year on the financial and business status of the firm. There is also a less comprehensive quarterly report called the 10-Q.

Ask Price (Offering Price): The price at which investors buy a security.

Asset: Anything having commercial value to a company or individual.

Balance Sheet: Lists the assets, liabilities, and equity of a corporation at a specific point in time. It's where you go to determine what the company is actually worth.

Bear Market: Opposite of a bull market. A market with prices going down over an extended period of time. Many people say that when key market indexes fall over 20 percent, it's a bear market.

Beta Rating: A measure of a stock's risk relative to the market, usually the Standard & Poor's 500 index. The market's beta is always 1.0. A beta higher than 1.0 indicates that on average, when the market rises, the stock will generally rise, and that when the market falls, the stock will generally fall. A beta lower than 1.0 indicates that on average, the stock will move to a lesser extent than the market. The higher the beta, the greater the risk.

Bid Price: The price at which an investor can sell a stock.

Blue Chip Stock: A reference to larger, established companies with track records of good earnings and dividends. IBM, for example, is a blue chip stock. Microsoft, on the other hand, is not because it doesn't pay a dividend.

Bond: An interest bearing certificate promising to pay interest and principal at specified times. They are usually issued by corporations and government agencies. Typically, investors try to diversify their investment portfolios with stocks *and* bonds, since the value of bonds typically moves inversely to the value of stocks.

Book Value: The value of a company after its liabilities have been deducted from its assets. Some people prefer to call it *net asset value.* It's considered one of the most controversial measurements in value investing, since some maintain book values can be outdated and are therefore not a good current measurement of a company's liquidating value.

Block Trade: A large quantity of stock, usually 10,000 shares or more.

Broker: Also stockbroker. An investment professional who is paid on commission for buying and selling securities.

Bull Market: Opposite of bear market. A stock market which is moving up in price.

Buy Stop Order: Used in placing a buy order, usually for covering a short position (see also Short Sale). The order establishes an absolute price level at which the investor will buy a stock, and it will not be bought until it reaches that price.

Capital Gains: The monetary gains on an investment when an investor sells and the principal has increased in value.

Capitalization: The total market value of a stock, determined by multiplying the number of shares times the market price.

Cash Flow: The amount of real money a company takes in. Free cash flow is the amount after all normal capital spending has occurred.

Churning: A trouble sign on your brokerage statement. Churning is excessive buying and selling of stocks. When initiated by a broker, it's usually done to generate commissions rather than for the client's well-being. It is, therefore, actionable, typically through arbitration.

Common Stock: The certificate of ownership in a publicly traded corporation.

Consolidated Statement: A report issued by a holding company which consolidates all of its subsidiaries' earnings, assets, and liabilities. It sometimes makes it tough to look at the results of individual operations.

Current Assets: All assets which are convertible into cash within one year.

Cyclical Stocks: Stocks in an industry such as automobiles, heavy construction equipment, and oil-drilling equipment, whose performance is closely tied to the condition of the general economy.

Dealer: An investment banking firm which underwrites stock issues and offers them to the public. The dealer usually will buy and sell the stock after the stock is trading. Since they represent shares of a given stock on the market, dealers have a stake in those shares rising, because it helps their profit.

Dilution: The effect new stock has on the stock of existing shareholders. When a company issues new stock, the same earnings must be distributed over more shares. However, if earnings are growing fast enough, at a rate that outpaces the amount of new stock, there is no dilution and a shareholder's investment may be worth more.

Discount Broker: A broker who will buy and sell securities but not offer investment advice; charges much less than a full-service broker.

Diversification: The technique of buying several different industries and several different stocks within each industry. It also involves buying investments other than stocks to diversify a portfolio, such as bonds, precious metals, or money market mutual funds. Diversification is a portfolio strategy to help diminish risk.

Dividend: A portion of earnings in the form of money or stock paid to an investor by a company. Not all stocks pay dividends, choosing to reinvest these earnings in the business so it can grow faster.

Dividend Payout Ratio: Annual dividends per share divided by annual earnings per share. See also *Yield.*

Dow Jones Industrial Average: Thirty stocks which represent different industries, each of which is a leader in its industry.

Earnings: The amount of money a company has left over after paying all of its bills and obligations. It may distribute a portion or all of the earnings to investors in the form of stock or cash dividends, or reinvest those earnings in the business to help it grow.

Earnings per Share (EPS):   The amount of money a company has after paying all obligations divided by the number of shares in the company.

Equity: The total assets of a company less all its debt equals the equity. It's similar to the amount of money you've paid into a mortgage. The amount that's paid off—with any addition in market value if you were to sell at that moment—is your equity in the home.

Extraordinary Item: A one-year event which affects the company's earnings for one quarter or year. Value investors look for these extraordinary items to signal whether the company is in for long-term problems that may depress the stock for a long time or just short-term problems that may depress the stock and provide a buying opportunity.

Fundamental Analysis: A method of stock analysis which relies on the reported numbers of a company for investment decisions, as opposed to technical analysis which looks at the price and volume history of a stock. It is one of the important factors of value investing.

Generally Accepted Accounting Principles (GAAP):   The financial reporting standards with which all public companies must comply so that each annual or quarterly report is uniform. Whenever a company strays from these principles or has to make a major restructuring of its results to fit them, it usually indicates problems or big changes in the company's financial fortunes. Any investor should pay attention when a company has to disclose any accounting change. It's not always bad, but it's not always good, either.

Goodwill: An intangible asset of a company, usually quantified when a company is purchased, the amount being the excess over book value. Always check to see what the company considers goodwill, because it's up to them to define what it is.

Growth Stock: A stock that represents new technology, a new service, or a new way of doing something. In financial terms, it often means a young company that is expanding quickly and is using earnings (if it has any) to grow the business rather than paying off shareholders in the form of cash or stock.

Income Statement (Profit & Loss Statement): Use it with the company's balance sheet in examining the overall financial fortunes of the company. It gives you the closest look at the reasons for a company's profit or loss and the revenue and expenses a company has.

Income Stock: A stock having a history of regular dividend payments that contribute the largest proportion of the stock's overall return. Generally, these stocks are considered low-risk and do not make wide swings in pricing.

Inflation: The rise in prices caused by an undue expansion in paper money or bank credit. Inflation is generally seen as bad for the stock market because:

1. Rising prices mean a slowdown in business. If something costs more, you either pay more or buy less. Most people buy less, which gives companies less business, which leads to fewer jobs, more unemployment, and even fewer people who can afford to buy things.

2. Rising prices mean rising interest rates. If a person or a company needs something and doesn't have the cash to buy it, they may need to use credit. More demand for credit means lenders can charge more for the limited money they have to lend out.

3. Rising interest rates hurt everyone. Well, almost everyone. If you've got money to lend, you're in great shape. But if a company or a person has to borrow, their net worth goes down. And if your net worth goes down, you're worth less, which means that companies with higher debt often trade lower because assets are offset by borrowings.

Initial Public Offering (IPO): The first offering of stock by a corporation to the public. Often called "going public," it allows a private company to price its worth in the marketplace and gather new funds for expansion. Investors interested in buying IPO shares should read the prospectus carefully to understand the company's earnings and assets.

Insiders: Corporate officers who own stock in the company. Insider trading, which got a bad name in the 1980s, is actually a very legal disclosure process wherein company officers and board members have to tell how many of the company's shares they've bought or sold when they do it. Insider trading becomes illegal when officers act without proper disclosure. Individual shareholders want to keep an eye on insider trading—often listed in most newspaper business sections—because it indicates what top management thinks the stock is worth. If a top manager is buying stock in his own company, that's a sign of confidence. If he's selling, it may be for two reasons: either he needs to change his personal investments (he may need to take profits for some personal reason) or he may believe the company's earnings and sales are heading down in the future, which may be a trigger for you to sell as well.

Institutional Investors: Pension funds, mutual funds, insurance companies, investment advisors, banks—any entity that manages a large pool of funds and chooses to invest it in the markets. Since there are so many institutional investors, they often have a considerable impact on a company's stock price when they buy or sell.

Intangible Assets: Assets without a strict dollar value, such as patents, trademarks, copyrights, and trade names. (See also *Goodwill*.)

Inventory: Goods made and held by a company for sale. If inventory keeps going up and sales don't, that's a problem, because it costs money to keep inventory warehoused. Inventory is necessary and favorable as long as you keep up with demand, but if you lose demand, then inventory is a burden.

Investment Banker: A firm which will commit its own capital to bring a company public. If there are not enough buyers for a new issue, the investment banker will buy the unsold shares and sell them out over time. (See also *Dealer*.)

Leverage: Using debt instead of equity to finance a company, an asset, or any corporate activity. If a company is taking on a lot of debt to finance its operations, make sure revenues are growing even faster so they can pay off the money without problems.

Leveraged Buyout (LBO):   The process of borrowing money to buy a company. It was big in the eighties, not done as often in the debt-conscious nineties.

Liabilities: What a company owes in the form of accounts payable, bank borrowings, or bond indebtedness.

Limit Order: An order to buy or sell a security at a specific price. It might be worthwhile putting a limit on a buy or sell price if you think the market could diminish your returns.

Liquid Asset: An asset that can be converted into cash within 30 days.

Liquidity: The degree of ease and certainty of value with which a security can be converted into cash.

Long: Ownership of a stock. When you own a stock, you are *long* the stock.

Margin: The ability to borrow money by pledging your stock as collateral.

Market Capitalization: The total dollar value of all securities issued by a company: preferred and common stocks, bonds, and debentures. When you look at market capitalization, you find out whether a stock is a small-capitalization (small-cap) or middle-capitalization (mid-cap) stock. You will sometimes hear of mutual funds investing in small-cap and mid-cap stocks. Generally, stocks with smaller market capitalizations tend to be younger growth stocks, but that is not always the case.

Market Order: An order to buy or sell stock at the current quoted prices.

NASDAQ: The National Association of Securities Dealers Automated Quotations system. When a security trades on NASDAQ, it trades between dealers who make a market in the stock, not on an exchange.

Net Income: The amount of income, or profit, after all the bills and obligations have been paid by a company.

New Issues: Securities being brought public for the first time. Corporations issue the securities through an investment banking firm, which sells them to the public. (See also *IPO.*)

Nonrecurring event: A one-time gain or loss to corporate earnings which is not part of the normal operating earnings of the firm. Another signal to value investors to take a look; nonrecurring events can sometimes lower the price of a stock.

Odd Lots: Quantities of less than 100 shares of a stock held by a single owner.

Over-the-Counter Market (OTC): See *NASDAQ.*

Penny Stocks: Stocks which sell typically for less than $1 a share. They are sold off of "pink sheets" at certain brokerages, not on any major exchange. Few become larger, more established companies.

Portfolio: A group of securities held by an investor.

Preferred Stock: A security representing prior claim over common stock to a firm's earnings and assets. Preferred stockholders normally forgo voting rights and receive a fixed dividend that takes precedence over payment of dividends to common stockholders.

Price-to-Book Ratio: Market price per share divided by book value (tangible assets less all liabilities) per share. This ratio is a measure of stock valuation relative to net assets. A high ratio might imply an over-valued situation; a low one might indicate an overlooked stock.

Price-to-Cash Flow Ratio: Price per share divided by cash flow per share. It's a measure of the market's expectations regarding a firm's future financial health. Provides an indication of relative value, similar to the price-to-earnings ratio.

Price-to-Earnings Ratio (P/E):   The price of a stock divided by the earnings, done on a per-share basis. The higher the P/E ratio, the lower the earnings are to support the stock price. Depending on an investor's strategy, the number of times a stock is selling against earnings may be a signal to buy or sell a stock. A low P/E for a stock compared with its peers might mean a lack of market interest in the shares, but a high P/E might indicate confidence that the stock will grow quickly. Example: A stock selling for $100 a share and earning $8 per share is selling at a price-to-earnings ratio of $12^{1}/_{2}$ to 1, or simply stated, $12^{1}/_{2}$. Meanwhile, a $100-a-share stock with earnings-per-share of $2 has a P/E of 50 to 1, or 50.

Price-to-Sales Ratio: Price per share divided by the latest 12-month sales per share. It's used similarly to price-to-earnings ratios to identify "out-of-favor" stocks.

Pro Forma Statement: A calculated guess of the future earnings or balance sheet of a company. Usually seen in initial public offering documents or merger and acquisition proposals.

Prospectus: Also known as a "red herring." The document investors receive on any new issue, which gives a full description of the company's past and future operations.

Public Offering: Stock issued by a company. If it is the first offering, it is called a primary or initial public offering. Most companies issue stock more than once.

Quick Ratio (Acid-Test Ratio):   Used for analyzing a balance sheet, and many companies include it. You get it by subtracting inventory from current assets and dividing by current liabilities. Also called the acid test ratio because it tells how much money is truly available for current needs. A quick ratio of at least 1 to 10 is usually considered satisfactory.

Quotation: The bid and offer (or ask) prices of a stock.

Real Rate of Return: The annual percentage return realized on an investment, adjusted for changes in the price level due to inflation or deflation.

Receivables: Money owed to a company which is payable within a specified time period.

Retained Earnings: The earnings a company keeps after paying interest, dividends, salaries, and all the bills.

Return on Assets (ROA): A way to assess how much a company earns on each dollar of assets in the business. ROA is found by dividing the earnings of a company by the assets required to make them. It allows you to see how efficiently a company uses its assets compared to others in its industry. Comparing this rate to the interest it pays on borrowed funds shows the extent of its financial *leverage* (see Leverage).

Return on Equity (ROE): Another way to assess a company's profitability compared with its competitors. ROE is found by dividing the earnings of a company by the equity. It measures how much the investors are making on their investment.

Revenues: Total sales of a company.

Reverse Split: Making many shares into a few. If a stock has a reverse split of one for ten, it means if you own one hundred shares before the split, you now own ten. If a company does a reverse split, it's usually because it wants to boost its stock price by leaving fewer shares out in the marketplace. The fewer shares there are to buy, the higher the price of those that are out there.

Round Lot: Usually one hundred shares of a stock. (See also *Odd Lots.*)

Securities and Exchange Commission (SEC): The governmental regulatory body which governs all securities and exchanges. It formulates rules for acceptable behavior on the part of Wall Street dealers and brokers and the exchanges. *SEC filings* are the essential financial and operational documents a public company must file with the government to be allowed to trade; companies must pledge the accuracy of all revenue, earnings, and shareholder documents they put on file. All these documents are available to the public, most easily through the EDGAR system at public libraries and on the Internet.

Securities Analyst: Someone who analyzes companies to determine their value as investments. They usually work out of stock brokerage houses or large institutions. Analysts are responsible for research reports that brokerages issue on stocks. *Warning:* Before you take an analyst's recommendation on a stock, check to see how much of that stock the brokerage owns. This information can typically be found in the company's 10K report, a more detailed version of the annual report. Many brokerages act as agents taking companies public, and they have a proprietary stake in maximizing the value of the stock. While most analysts are objective and thorough in their decision making, it's always good to check what stake that brokerage has when issuing a report.

Shareholders' Equity: The value of a company after all other liabilities are deducted from assets. It's the amount which is owned by investors.

Short Sale: Selling stock you don't own (especially borrowing shares from a broker) in the hope that the stock price will go down, so that when you pay for the stock, you do it at the lower price. Short-sellers are investors who are betting on a speedy stock drop, and are therefore not long-term investors. Few value investors do short-selling; it doesn't fit their philosophy.

Small-Cap Stocks: Usually stocks which have a market capitalization of less than one billion dollars. Again, market capitalization is the total value of all securities issued by the company at par (an arbitrary stock price decided by the company's directors) or the face value of the bonds and debentures. Generally, the label is used to identify a group of stocks which are new, smaller, and more risky than the large-cap or blue chip stocks.

Speculation: Investing strategies which, according to value investing guru Benjamin Graham, do not promise safety of principal and an adequate return.

Split: When a stock splits, it increases the quantity of stock outstanding by a specific number, such as two shares for every one held by the investors. The company actually issues more shares and sends them to the current holders of the stock. Companies issue stock to add funds to their coffers for expansion. (See also *Reverse Split* and *Dilution.*)

Standard & Poor's 500: An index of 500 stocks which is a broad representation of the stock market when compared to the thirty stocks of the Dow Jones industrial average.

Stock Dividend: A stock payment received from a company. Often issued to investors when a company does not have the cash to pay a dividend.

Street Name: A stock certificate registered in the name of a Wall Street firm which holds the certificate for the customer who owns the shares. Facilitates the buying and selling of stock. If stock is not held in street name, it must be endorsed by the owner of the stock when it is sold, a cumbersome, often time-consuming process.

Technical Analysis: A method of analyzing stocks based on their previous prices and volume. It's a discipline that doesn't look at the company's management, recent news, or other factors that value investors depend on.

Total-Debt-to-Total-Asset Ratio: Short-term and long-term debt divided by total assets of the firm. A measure of a company's financial risk that indicates how much of the assets of the firm have been financed by debt.

Trader: Any person who buys and sells securities for short-term profits. Investors, by contrast, do thorough analysis and have a high regard for the safety of principal.

Transaction Costs: The commissions paid for buying and selling securities. When buying shares, keep track of these for tax purposes.

Value Line Index: An index representing 1700 companies from the New York and American Stock Exchanges and the over-the-counter market. It is an equal-weighted index, which means all of the 1700 stocks, regardless of market price or total market value, are weighted equally.

Wilshire 5000 Equity Index: A stock market measure comprising 5000 equity securities. It includes all New York Stock Exchange and American Stock Exchange issues and the most active over-the-counter issues. The index represents the total dollar value of all 5000 stocks.

Working Capital: The excess of a company's current assets over its current liabilities, that is, cash plus accounts receivable plus inventory minus the sum of accounts payable plus accrued liabilities and short-term loans. This measurement tells you whether a company can meet its obligations, expand its sales volume, and take advantage of favorable investments like mergers or the purchase of an attractive new product line for its business.

Yield: The ratio of return on any investment, expressed as a percentage. For example, a stock bought at $100 that pays a dividend of $5 per year is said to yield (or have a dividend yield) of 5 percent (5 divided by 100).

Mutual Fund Terms

Alpha: Alpha is a measure of the difference between a fund's actual returns and its expected performance, given its level of risk as measured by beta. A positive alpha figure indicates the fund has performed better than its beta would predict. A negative alpha indicates the fund's under-performance, given the expectations established by the fund's beta.

Annual Report: Mutual funds are required to publish and distribute upon demand annual reports twice a year. The reports list stock and bond holdings, sales and purchases, as well as letters from fund managers.

Automatic Reinvestment Plan: A plan offered by a mutual fund in which the fund automatically reinvests all distributions to a shareholder account.

Balanced Fund: A mutual fund that combines investments in common stock, bonds, and preferred stock. Its goal is to provide income plus some capital appreciation.

Beta: Beta is a measure of a fund's sensitivity to market movements. By definition, the beta of the benchmark index is 1.00. A fund with a 1.50

beta is expected to perform 50 percent better than the index in up markets and 50 percent worse in down markets. Beta is calculated by Morningstar over the trailing 36-month period.

Capital Gain: An increase in the value of a capital asset such as common stock. If the asset is sold, the gain is a *realized* capital gain. A capital gain may be short-term (one year or less) or long-term (more than one year.)

Closed-End Fund: A mutual fund which issues a set number of shares which are then traded on an exchange.

Deferred Load: Deferred loads, or class B shares, as the name implies, are paid when an investor leaves the fund. The load usually diminishes over time. For example, a fund may have a deferred load of 5 percent. The load may decrease by 1 percent a year. At the end of the fifth year, the class B shares would be exchanged for class A shares and there would be no redemption fee.

Dollar Cost Averaging (DCA):   DCA is the process of investing equal dollar amounts on a fixed schedule no matter what the market condition or the outlook. When you practice DCA, you buy more shares when prices are low and fewer shares when prices are high. This gives you a cost basis that reflects the fund's average NAV. It also protects against investing a lump sum at a market peak. DCA is most suitable for the long-term investor who seeks to accumulate wealth by religiously plowing money into the market.

Exchange Privilege: A feature offered by a mutual fund in which a shareholder is able to move money between various funds at a very minimal processing charge and without a commission.

Expense Ratio: Many investors consider the expense ratio to be the most important aspect of a mutual fund. Returns aren't guaranteed; expenses are. If expenses are a key aspect of your fund selection, you may want to consider an index fund. Index funds typically have expense ratios in the neighborhood of 0.20 to 0.30 percent a year. A fund's expense ratio is the total percent of assets deducted from a fund each year (the fees are in very small amounts on a daily basis). Expense ratios vary greatly from fund to fund. Vanguard, well known as one of the fund industry's frugal funds, carries a median expense ratio of 0.25 percent.

Family of Funds: A group of mutual funds under the same management company, such as Vanguard or Fidelity.

Front Load: A front load is nothing more than a commission paid to the broker who sold you the fund. There is no shame in paying a load, provided you receive sound financial advice and good service. If you need these features, then a load fund may be the way to go. Front loads range from 0.40 percent up to 9.00 percent. If you purchase a fund with a front load of 4.00 percent, for every dollar you invest, 4 cents is deducted. Funds with front loads are usually denoted as class A shares. Front loads usually decline as an investor invests more dollars in a fund.

Fund Fees: There's no such thing as a free lunch. Just as brokers get paid a commission when you buy and sell stocks and market makers pocket the bid and ask spreads, mutual funds charge fees that are deducted from the fund's assets. Various types of fees are sprinkled throughout this glossary.

Index Fund: A portfolio of stocks held by a mutual fund designated to track with a market index, such as an S&P 500 fund.

Investment Style: All funds have a stated investment objective to which they must adhere. Equity, or stock, funds are considered growth, value, or a blend. Morningstar takes a stock portfolio's average price/earnings ratio (PE), relative to the average of the S&P 500 Index, and adds to it the portfolio's average price/book (PB) figure, relative to that of the S&P 500. Funds with a combined relative PE and PB figure of less than 1.75 are considered value funds. Portfolios with combined ratios from 1.75 to 2.25 are considered blend funds (by definition, the S&P 500 scores 2.00), and any funds with a sum greater than 2.25 are classified as growth funds.

Level Loads: Level-load funds, or C shares, often charge small front loads, small deferred loads, and have higher than normal expense ratios. Unlike class B shares, level-load funds don't always convert to A shares after a set period of time.

Load: A sales commission to buyers that a mutual fund may charge. About 60 percent of all funds are loaded. There is not a correlation between load and performance. Just because a fund charges a load or is sold by a broker does not imply it is a good fund.

Low-Load Fund: A mutual fund that charges a small commission for investment.

Market Capitalization: Funds are broken into three market-cap classifications: Large-cap = $5 billion–$25 billion; mid-cap = $1 billion–$5 billion; small-cap = $250 million–$1 billion.

Median Market Cap: The average market capitalization (share price $\times$ number of shares outstanding) of the companies a fund holds. Half of the fund's assets are invested in stocks that have market caps larger than the fund's median market cap, and half of the fund's assets are invested in companies that have market caps smaller than the fund's median market cap.

Money Market Mutual Fund: A mutual fund that invests in very short-term financial securities, usually of less than 30 days maturity.

Mutual Fund: A pool of investors' money invested and managed by an investment advisor. Money can be invested in the fund or withdrawn at any time, with few restrictions, at net asset value (the per share market value of all securities held), minus any loads and/or fees.

Net Asset Value: The net asset value, or NAV, is the price of one share of a mutual fund. It is determined daily by dividing the total net assets of a fund by the total number of shares. For example, if the net assets of the fund are $1 million and the fund has 100,000 shares outstanding, the NAV is $10. No-load funds are purchased and sold at NAV. Front-end loads are bought at the NAV less the load.

No-Load Fund: A mutual fund that sells its shares at net asset value, without the addition of a sales fee (load).

Open-End Investment Company: A mutual fund which issues shares when investors want to buy into the fund, as opposed to a closed-end fund, which has a stated number of shares.

Portfolio Manager: The individual responsible for managing large pools of funds. Insurance companies, mutual funds, bank trusts departments, pension funds, and other institutional investors may employ portfolio managers.

Prospectus: A description of the fund's investment policies and objectives. Included in the prospectus are descriptions of the types of securities the fund invests in, such as common stocks or municipal obligations, plus any investment parameters. While prospectuses are generally dull to read, they do serve a purpose. The fund's objectives and expenses are clearly defined. Beware: Don't be swayed by pretty graphs or glossy pictures. In fact, be wary of plush prospectuses. They are printed at the expense of existing shareholders. Shareholders should prefer their fund cut expenses and publish no-frills prospectuses.

Redemption Fees: Charges assessed upon redemption of mutual fund shares.

Return: Consists of income plus capital gains relative to investment.

R-Squared: R-squared reflects the percentage of a fund's movements that are explained by movements in its benchmark index (the S&P 500 Index is the benchmark used by Morningstar for all stock funds; the Lehman Brothers Aggregate Index is the benchmark used for all bond funds). An R-squared of 100 for a fund indicates that all movements of a fund are completely explained by movements in the index. A fund must have an R-squared of 75 or higher for its beta and alpha to be considered reliable.

Standard Deviation: A statistical measurement of dispersion about an average, which for a mutual fund depicts how widely the returns varied over a certain period of time. If a fund has a high standard deviation, the predicted range of performance is wide, implying greater volatility. Standard deviation is most appropriate as a measurement when looking at a single fund. The figure cannot be combined for more than one fund because the standard deviation for a portfolio of multiple funds is not the sum of its parts.

Tax Efficiency: Tax consideration is often ignored, especially when investment strategies that require frequent trading are discussed. Tax efficiency is a measure of how well a fund avoids making distributions in the form of capital gains and dividends. Unless you sell a fund, the only taxes you pay with a mutual fund are on fund distributions. There are two ways a fund can generate distributions (1) by selling stocks or bonds for a gain, or (2) by holding stocks or bonds that pay dividends or interest. Given this, funds that do not trade actively or hold smaller, non-yielding stocks tend to be the most tax-efficient funds. The median expense ratio for all funds is exactly 1.00 percent.

Total Return: For a no-load fund, total return is merely the percentage return over a given time, typically 1 month, 3 months, 12 months, 3 years, 5 years, 10 years, and 15 years. Total return includes yearly fund expenses, but it does not include loads. Load funds are often recorded unadjusted for a load. Keep in mind that when you view total returns for load funds, the actual return experienced by shareholders is less than reported.

Turnover: A measure of a fund's trading activity. A high turnover ratio—above 100 percent—implies an aggressive investment approach. A low turnover ratio indicates a buy-and-hold strategy. A turnover of 100 percent does not necessarily indicate that all securities in the portfolio have been traded. In practical terms, the resulting percentage loosely represents the percentage of the portfolio's holdings that have changed over the past year. Turnover can, but does not always, give a good indication of a fund's tax efficiency. Buy and hold is the most tax-friendly scenario. If taxes are a consideration, select funds with low turnover ratios.

I2b-I Fees: The 12b is a marketing fee and is one of the most obscure and difficult fees to understand. 12b-1s pay largely for a fund's marketing expenses. Most seasoned mutual fund investors seek funds that are not the toast of Wall Street. They seek undiscovered gems with small asset bases. 12b-1 fees do nothing more than promote a fund, the exact opposite of what a fund investor desires. They are reported as separate entities, but in fact are included in a fund's expense ratio. 12b-1 fees are capped at 1.00 percent.

Value Cost Averaging (VCA):   While DCA is the process of investing fixed dollar amounts regardless of market conditions, VCA is the process of investing for a fixed portfolio value. Suppose your goal is to increase your mutual fund worth by $100 a month. If, after one month, your fund does not gain value, you add $100. If the next month your fund gains $100, you add nothing. If, after the following month, your fund rises $200, you redeem $100. VCA is aimed at investing when prices fall or are flat, holding steady when prices rise, and taking some off the table when the market scorches. Unfortunately, the market doesn't follow a perfect pattern. The market could rise and rise and rise for years on end. This would lead the participant in VCA to stockpile cash that could have been invested at a much lower value at an earlier time. VCA may also involve considerable buying and selling during times of heightened volatility, increasing the tax burden and fees. VCA is most appropriate for risk-adverse investors with little concern for taxes. It works best in a choppy market.

While fund fees appear to be complex, they are quite simple. For a no-load fund, the total yearly expense is represented in the expense ratio.

While VCA is not a foolproof system, it does provide investors with discipline—an attribute lacking in all but the most successful investors.

With class C you avoid the steep up-front fees and the large deferred load, but you are stuck with a higher yearly expense ratio.

Avoid C shares that do not have a conversion feature to A shares. The high yearly fees will level your returns.

Sources: American Association of Individual Investors; Christine Ammer and Dean Ammer, *Dictionary of Business and Economics,* Free Press, New York, 1984; Sage Investments, via America Online.

Your Government at Work
How to Make Sense of SEC Filings

You say 10K, I say 10Q…let's call the whole thing off. Not so fast. You need this stuff. There used to be a time, back in the dark ages (about five years ago), when you had to beg your chosen company's investor relations department for government filings that contained a lot more information than you could get in the glossy annual report. Then you had to wait by the mailbox for days for it to arrive.

No more. With the click of a button, you can receive hard copies immediately of virtually any public company's filings with the Securities and Exchange Commission, the government's top watchdog agency for investors.

One of the best online sources for SEC data on companies is Disclosure Inc. (http://www.disclosure.com), which lists all documents that publicly traded companies are required to release to shareholders and file with the government. America Online has a special link to the resource as well. You can also go to the Securities and Exchange Commission website (http://www.sec.gov), but it takes a little longer to get where you're going.

Meantime, here's a description from Disclosure Inc. of the major SEC documents shareholders should be familiar with and what types of information they contain.

The 10K

This is the juicier version of the annual report you read about in Chapter 4. The 10K has to be filed with the SEC within 90 days after the company closes its business year. Its contents are as follows.

COVER PAGE

Lists the fiscal year end, state or other jurisdiction of incorporation or organization, title of each class of security and the exchange on which it is registered, and the number of shares outstanding of each of the issuer's classes of common stock, as of the latest practicable date, which is commonly the filing date, *not* the time period covered in the document.

PART I

Item 1—Business.   Identifies principal products and services of the company and principal markets and methods of distribution. If "material," it also identifies competitive factors; backlog and expectation of fulfillment; availability of raw materials; importance of patents, licenses, and franchises; estimated cost of research; number of employees; and effects of compliance with environmental laws. If there is more than one line of business, a statement is included for each of the last three years. The statement includes total sales and net income for each line which, during either of the last two fiscal years, accounted for 10 percent or more of total sales or pretax income.

Item 2—Properties.   Location and character of principal plants, mines, and other important properties and whether they are held in fee or leased.

Item 3—Legal proceedings.   Brief description of material legal proceedings pending.

Item 4—Submission of matters to be voted on by security holders. This is a preliminary agenda of voting issues for the annual meeting or any special shareholders meeting called by the company's management.

PART II

Item 5—Market for the registrant's common stock and related security holder matters.   Includes principal market in which voting securities are traded, with high and low sales prices (in the absence thereof, the range of bid and asked quotations for each quarterly period during the past two years) and the dividends paid during the past two years. In addition to the frequency and amount of dividends paid, this item contains a discussion concerning future dividends.

Item 6—Selected financial data.   These are five-year selected data, including net sales and operating revenue; income or loss from continuing operations, both total and per common share; total assets; long-term obligations, including redeemable preferred stock; and cash dividend declared per common share. These data also include additional items that could enhance understanding of trends in financial condition and results of operations. Furthermore, the effects of inflation and changing prices should be reflected in the five-year summary.

Item 7—Management's discussion and analysis of financial condition and results of operations.   Under broad guidelines, this includes liquidity, capital resources, and results of operations; trends that are favorable or unfavorable as well as significant events or uncertainties; causes of any material changes in the financial statements as a whole; limited data concerning subsidiaries; and discussion of the effects of inflation and changing prices.

Item 8—Financial statements and supplementary data.   Two-year audited balance sheets as well as three-year audited statements of income and cash flow.

Item 9—Changes in and disagreements with accountants on accounting and financial disclosure.   See why they're disagreeing. It could be very interesting.

PART III

Item 10—Directors and executive officers.   Name, office, term of office, and specific background data on each.

Item 11—Remuneration of directors and officers.   List of each director and highest paid officers with aggregate annual remuneration exceeding $40,000. Also includes the total paid all officers and directors as a group. Also lists bonuses and stock options awarded. This is particularly interesting information if you think the company may be ripe for a takeover. Some companies structure pay to benefit executives if they think a takeover or merger might happen.

Item 12—Security ownership of certain beneficial owners and management. Identification of owners of 5 percent or more of registrant's stock. Also lists the amount and percent of each class of stock held by officers and directors.

Item 13—Certain relationships and related transactions. A place for extraordinary transactions made during the year.

PART IV

Item 14—Exhibits, financial statement schedules, and reports on Form 8K. Complete, audited annual financial information and a list of exhibits filed. Also, any unscheduled material events or corporate changes filed in an 8K (see page 144) during the year.

FORM 10K SCHEDULES (WHEN APPLICABLE)

1. Investments other than investments in affiliates

2. Receivables from related parties and underwriters, promoters, and employees other than affiliates

3. Condensed financial information

4. Indebtedness of affiliates (not current)

5. Property, plant, and equipment

6. Accumulated depreciation, depletion, and amortization of property, plant, and equipment

7. Guarantees of securities of other issuers

8. Valuation and qualifying accounts

9. Short-term borrowings

10. Supplementary income statement information

11. Supplementary profit and loss information

12. Income from dividends (equity in net profit and loss of affiliates)

The 10Q

This is the quarterly financial report filed by most companies. Although unaudited, it provides a continuing view of a company's financial position during the year. The 10Q report must be filed 45 days after close of fiscal year quarter.

COVER PAGE

Lists time period represented; state of incorporation; former name; address and fiscal year if changed since last report; whether the registrant filed any 1934 Act reports during the past 12 months and has been subject to such filing requirements for the past 90 days; whether the registrant has filed all documents and reports required under the Securities Exchange Act of 1934 subsequent to the distribution of securities; and the number of shares outstanding of each of the company's classes of common stock as of the last practicable date (commonly the filing date, *not* the time period covered in the document).

PART I

Item 1—Quarterly financial statements.

Item 2—Management discussion and analysis of material changes in the amount of revenue and expense items.   Done in relation to previous quarters. Includes the effect of any changes in accounting principles.

PART II

Item 3—Legal proceedings.   Brief description of material legal proceedings pending. When civil rights or environmental statutes are involved, proceedings must be disclosed.

Item 4—Changes in securities.   Material changes in the rights of holders of any class of registered security.

Item 5—Defaults upon senior securities.   Material defaults in the payment of principal, interest, sinking fund or purchase fund installment, dividend, or other material default not cured within 30 days.

Item 6—Submission of matters to be voted on by security holders. Information related to the convening of a meeting of shareholders, whether annual or special, and the matters voted upon, with particular emphasis on the election of directors.

Item 7—Other materially important events. Information on any other item of interest to shareholders not already provided for in this form or reported in an 8K.

Item 8—Exhibits and reports on Form 8K. Any unscheduled material events or corporate changes reported in an 8K during the prior quarter.

Form 8K

This is a report of unscheduled material events or corporate changes deemed of importance to the shareholders or to the SEC. Items 1–3 and 8 must be reported in an 8K within fifteen days of the event. Items 4 and 6 must be filed within five business days after the event. Item 5 is optional, meaning there is no mandatory time for filing.

Item 1—Changes in control of registrant. Means that the company is being taken over or a merger is pending.

Item 2—Acquisition or disposition of assets. Describes what is being bought or sold.

Item 3—Bankruptcy or receivership. Details of said court filings.

Item 4—Changes in registrant's certifying accountant. If a company changes accountants, it's important to know why. There may be irregularities that affect future results and the overall value of the stock.

Item 5—Other materially important events. Anything that relates to the future direction of the company.

Item 6—Resignation of registrant's directors. Another important "why" question. If directors are leaving, do they have a reason that might affect future results?

Item 7—Financial statements and/or exhibits. This may contain preliminary financial details and forecasts for the acquisition, merger, or restructuring the company is reporting. It's another key to future results, which affects value.

Item 8—Change in fiscal year. If a company changes its reporting periods, it requires a restructuring of the way it accounts for past and future results.

Proxy Statement

A proxy statement provides official notification to designated classes of shareholders of matters to be brought to a vote at a shareholders' meeting. Proxy votes may be solicited for changing the company officers and many other matters. Disclosures normally made via a proxy statement may in some cases be made using Part III of Form 10K.

Prospectus

When the sale of securities as proposed in an "offering" registration statement is approved by the SEC, any changes required by the SEC are incorporated into the prospectus. This document must be made available to investors before the sale of the security is initiated. It also contains the actual offering price, which may have been changed after the registration statement was approved.

Disclosure normally made via a proxy statement may in some cases be made using Part III of Form 10K.

Notes

Chapter 1

1. Janet Lowe, *Warren Buffett Speaks: Wit and Wisdom from the World's Greatest Investor,* John Wiley & Sons, New York, 1997, p. 100.

2. Interview with Barbara Bowles, founder and president of the Kenwood Group, Chicago, IL, Aug. 11, 1998.

3. Peter Lynch, *One Up on Wall Street,* Simon & Schuster, Penguin Books, New York, 1990, p. 156.

4. Benjamin Graham and David Dodd, *Security Analysis,* McGraw-Hill, New York, 1940.

5. Benjamin Graham, *The Intelligent Investor,* Harper & Row, New York, 1973, p. 101.

6. Ibid., pp. 103–104.

7. Warren Buffett, chairman of Omaha-based Berkshire Hathaway Corp., is one of the nation's wealthiest individuals. With Vice Chairman

Charles Munger, Buffett Pilots Berkshire Hathaway, a conglomeration of businesses that Buffett bought in 1965 and built on Benjamin Graham's value principles. Before that, he was manager of a fund called the Buffett Partnership. In *Warren Buffett Speaks* it was noted that investors who gave Buffett $10,000 to manage in 1956, the year he started Buffett Partnership, and kept reinvesting all profits back into his now-closed partnership, would now have fortunes in excess of $80 million apiece (p. 4).

Chapter 2

1. Hewitt Associates, Riverwoods, IL, "The Hewitt 401(k) Index," www.hewittassoc.com.

2. Lowe, *Warren Buffett Speaks,* p. 100.

3. Telephone interview by author, Sept. 2, 1998.

4. Telephone interview by author, Sept. 1, 1998.

5. Bowles: referring to current market situation, Sept. 1, 1998.

6. Telephone interview by author, Aug. 31, 1998.

7. Ken Kurson, "Here's a Look at the Five-Day Forecast, and…Sweet Mother of God!" *Esquire,* October 1998, p. 99.

8. Telephone interview by author, Sept. 9, 1998.

9. Telephone interview by author, Sept. 3, 1998.

Chapter 3

1. Graham, *The Intelligent Investor,* p. 82.

2. Lowe, *Warren Buffett Speaks,* p. 100.

3. Janet Lowe, *Value Investing Made Easy,* McGraw-Hill, New York, 1996, p. 36.

4. Graham, *The Intelligent Investor,* p. 273.

5. American Association of Individual Investors, Stock Selection Guide, Chicago, 1994 (listed on website, www.aaii.org).

Chapter 4

1. Lowe, *Warren Buffett Speaks,* p. 114.
2. Graham, *The Intelligent Investor,* pp. 184–185.

Chapter 6

1. Graham, *The Intelligent Investor,* p. 63.
2. Telephone interview by author, Sept. 2, 1998.
3. Telephone interview by author, Aug. 31, 1998.

Chapter 8

1. Federal Trade Commission, Project Roadblock announcement, Jan. 30, 1996.

Chapter 9

1. "Computerized Investing FAQ's," American Association of Individual Investors website, (http://www.aaii.org).
2. Gregg Keizer, CNet network (www.cnet.com), Sept. 21, 1998.
3. National Association of Securities Dealers, 1998.

Chapter 11

1. Jane Bryant Quinn, *Making the Most of Your Money,* Simon & Schuster, New York, 1991, p. 486.

2. Vanguard Marketing Corporation, Vanguard Retirement Planning website (www.vanguard.com), 1998.

Chapter 12

1. Lowe, *Warren Buffett Speaks,* p. 98.

INDEX

ABOUT THE AUTHOR

Lisa Holton is a business writer whose work has appeared in the *Chicago Tribune, Better Homes and Gardens Family Money*, and *Nation's Business*. The former business editor of the *Chicago Sun-Times*, Holton covered personal finance and banking topics for the paper and created MoneyLife, the *Sun-Times* personal finance section. She is a national board member of the Society of American Business Editors and Writers (SABEW).